FOLK ARTS OF
WASHINGTON STATE

A Survey of Contemporary Folk Arts and

Artists in the State of Washington

Otto Oja of Cathlamet is a retired bucker and faller whose parents immigrated to the Northwest from Finland. During the early 1960s, he saw his first chainsaw carving. Today he demonstrates chainsaw carving at logging shows, and his pieces are on display at logging supply stores and in logging company offices in southwest Washington. He specializes in scenes from the woods, such as local wildlife, but his most characteristic pieces are representations of working loggers.

FOLK ARTS OF WASHINGTON STATE

A Survey of Contemporary Folk Arts and Artists in the State of Washington

Edited by Jens Lund
with Elizabeth Simpson

Contributors:

Harry Gammerdinger
Janet C. Gilmore
Phyllis A. Harrison
Jens Lund

 **Washington State Folklife Council**

TUMWATER, WASHINGTON

Folk Arts of Washington State is a "Project of Statewide Significance" officially sponsored and funded by the Washington State Centennial Commission.

Major grantors include the National Endowment for the Arts—Folk Arts Division, the Littlefield Foundation, and the Washington State Arts Commission.

For additional information, please contact the Washington State Folklife Council, 7510 Armstrong St. S.W., Tumwater, WA 98501, (206) 586-8252.

Library of Congress Cataloging-in-Publication Data

Folk arts of Washington State.

    Includes bibliographical references.
    1. Folk art—Washington (State) 2. Ethnic art—Washington (State) 3. Folk artists—Washington (State)—Biography. I. Lund, Jens, 1946-   . II. Simpson, Elizabeth, 1951-   . III. Gammerdinger, Harry.
NK835.W37F65 1989   745'.09797   89-16696
ISBN 0-9623539-0-6

Production, design, coordination, copy editing, and consulting services provided by Laing Communications Inc., Bellevue, Washington, affiliated with Vernon Publications Inc.

Front Cover: *Seed-art collage-mural by Elsie Koehler Johnson depicting the Andrew and Annie Koehler family homestead in Molson, Okanogan County.* (Photo by Jens Lund.)

Back Cover: *Elsie Koehler Johnson and her seed-art collage-mural.* (Photo by Jens Lund.)

CONTENTS

CONTRIBUTORS   vii

THE WASHINGTON STATE FOLKLIFE COUNCIL   ix

FOREWORD
by Jean Gardner, Co-Chair, Washington State Centennial Commission   xi

PREFACE
by Jens Lund   xiii

ACKNOWLEDGMENTS   xv

MAP OF WASHINGTON: PLACES CITED   xviii

INTRODUCTION: WHAT ARE THE FOLK ARTS OF
    WASHINGTON STATE?
by Jens Lund   1

"ISN'T THAT SOMETHING EVERYBODY KNOWS?":
    FOLK ART AND COMMUNITY
by Phyllis Harrison   53

MAKING SOMETHING OUT OF "NOTHING"
by Janet C. Gilmore   67

HONORING WORK: OCCUPATIONAL FOLK ART
    IN WASHINGTON
by Harry Gammerdinger   79

BIBLIOGRAPHY   92

APPENDIX: ETHNIC RESOURCE GUIDE
Compiled by Scott Nagel, Director, Northwest Folklife Festival   96

INDEX   103

PHOTO CREDITS   108

Floyd Broadbent of Naches, one of the Northwest's leading wildlife carvers and painters, learned his skills as a boy in upstate New York . The carved birds are less than an inch long.

CONTRIBUTORS

Harry Gammerdinger, Ph.D., is staff folklorist at the Center for Southern Folklore in Memphis, Tennessee, and a filmmaker. He wrote his doctoral dissertation on the making of documentary films by folklorists. Dr. Gammerdinger was one of the contract field researchers for the Folklife Council's 1987 folk art survey. He also worked on a similar project in Idaho and contributed to *Folk Art of Idaho: "We Came to Where We Were Supposed to Be."*

Janet C. Gilmore, Ph.D., was born in Portland, Oregon and grew up in Eugene. Granddaughter of Washington naval architect H.C. Hanson, she specializes in maritime folklife research. Dr. Gilmore is the author of *The World of the Oregon Fish Boat: A Folklife Study* and *A Catalog of Boat Catalogs*, and contributed to *From Hardanger to Harleys: A Survey of Wisconsin Folk Art*. Dr. Gilmore works as a freelance folklife researcher and was a field researcher for the 1987 folk art survey. She lives in Mt. Horeb, Wisconsin.

Phyllis A. Harrison, Ph.D., is a native and resident of Tacoma. Formerly folk arts coordinator for the Arvada Center in Denver, Colorado, she is now program director for the Institute of the NorthAmerican West in Fort Steilacoom. Her doctoral dissertation was on auctioneering in the southern Midwest and she is co-author of a study of the semiotics of Brazilian nonverbal communication. Dr. Harrison was also a contract researcher for the 1987 Washington folk art survey.

Jens Lund, Ph.D., has been Washington State Folklorist and Director of Folklife Programs for the Washington State Folklife Council since 1984. He is a native of Denmark and grew up in Connecticut. Dr. Lund worked for nine years as a freelance folklife researcher in fifteen states, and taught at Indiana University and the University of Washington. He wrote his doctoral dissertation on the folklife of Ohio River Valley fishermen.

Elizabeth Simpson teaches in the Interdisciplinary Writing Program at the University of Washington. She is a regional editor of *Northwest Folklore* and collaborating editor of *Nordic Folklore: Recent Studies*. Ms. Simpson has published articles on folklore and literature, and on the folklore of the Mt. St. Helens eruption. She is currently completing a dissertation on Northwest writer Ivan Doig.

Publications Committee of the Washington State Folklife Council: Patsy Callaghan, D.A.; Henning Sehmsdorf, Ph.D.; Dell Skeels, Ph.D.; Henry-York Steiner, Ph.D.; Nancy Worden; Scott Nagel; Marlys Swenson Waller. ❖

The Hutterite Brethren are a German-speaking sect with origins in the early Protestant Reformation. They live in communal agricultural settlements in the United States and Canada. Each colony has a master cabinetmaker. John Gross of the Marlin Colony, near Moses Lake, made this rocking chair.

THE WASHINGTON STATE FOLKLIFE COUNCIL

THE WASHINGTON STATE FOLKLIFE COUNCIL was founded in Yakima, Washington in 1983 to research, preserve, and present the culture of the State of Washington. With matching grants from the Washington State Arts Commission, the National Endowment for the Arts—Folk Arts Division, and the Washington Commission for the Humanities, the Council hired its first director in 1984. It was chartered as a nonprofit corporation in 1985, and moved to its present location in Tumwater in 1987. The Council publishes a quarterly newsletter, *The WashBoard*. The presidents/board chairs of the Council have been Frank Ferrel (1983-84), Penn Fix (1984-86), Richard Scholtz (1986-87), Henry-York Steiner (1987-88), and Diane M. Ellison (1988-present). For more information, please contact the Washington State Folklife Council, 7510 Armstrong St. S.W., Tumwater, WA 98501, (206) 586-8252.

Board of Directors, 1989

Diane M. Ellison, President/Chair, Aberdeen
Henry-York Steiner, Ph.D., Vice-Chair, Cheney
Scott Nagel, Treasurer, Seattle
Marlys Swenson Waller, Recording Secretary, Lopez Island
Carlton Appelo, Deep River
Marjorie Bangs Bennett, Ph.D., Bainbridge Island
Marilyn Bentz, Ph.D., Manchester
Susan Dwyer-Shick, Ph.D., J.D., Parkland
Lynne Masland, Bellingham
Representative Dick Nelson, Seattle
Alice Nugent, Seattle
Henning Sehmsdorf, Ph.D., Seattle
Dell Skeels, Ph.D., Seattle
Bud Stewart, Royal City
Agnes Tulee, Toppenish
Susan Winegardner, Spokane
Nancy Worden, Seattle

Staff

Jens Lund, Ph.D., Washington State Folklorist and Director of Folklife Programs
James Rosengren, Administrative Director
Della Jakasovic, Administrative Staff/Work Study
Melinda Clemensen and Cynthia La Mere, Archivist Interns

Uncle Sam is perched on a platform of laubsägerarbeit, *an intricate German form of scroll-sawing made by Otto Franz Stieber of Lynden. He learned the technique as a boy in Hamm, Germany.*

FOREWORD

by Jean Gardner, Co-Chair, Washington State Centennial Commission

From the wheatfields of the Palouse to the rain forests of the Olympic Peninsula, from a cattle ranch of the Big Bend to a Scandinavian neighborhood in Seattle, the State of Washington is remarkable for the diversity of its people. Some, such as the Hispanic-Americans of the Yakima Valley, share a common ethnic origin. Others, such as the loggers of Morton, share a common occupational base. Still others, such as the Native Americans in the fishing village of LaPush, share both a common origin and a common economy.

This wonderful diversity is represented in the special talents of Washington's folk artists. Some of these men and women learn their skills from older members of their family or community, others are self-taught, but all express the shared aesthetic sense of their people. These artists are carvers, painters, craftspeople, poets, needleworkers, singers, and storytellers, taking inspiration from their everyday lives.

Until recently, Washington paid little attention to the folk arts that flourish within its borders. But since the establishment of the Washington State Folklife Council in 1983, researchers have scoured the state from Asotin to Neah Bay looking for examples of art and artists who embody their communities' folk aesthetics. The results have been impressive, culminating in the 1988-1989 Governor's Invitational Art Exhibition: "'For As Long As I Can Remember . . .,' The Folk Art of Washington State." This touring exhibit, sponsored by the Washington State Folklife Council and the Washington State Capital Museum, was shown in Olympia, Seattle, Yakima, Spokane, Wenatchee, Anacortes, and Ephrata. This book, funded in part by a "Projects of Statewide Significance" grant from the Washington State Centennial Commission, gives the reader a look at some of Washington's folk artists and the roles they play in their communities.

Washingtonians have much to be proud of in this Centennial year. Thanks to the work of the Washington State Folklife Council, we can now celebrate the greatness of our folk artists, as well. ❖

Dean Curtis of Dean's Muffler and Brake Shop in Ellensburg made this horseshoe-pitcher out of mufflers, exhaust pipe, and brake rotors.

PREFACE

by Jens Lund

"Folk art in Washington? How can this be? The place is too new. Aside from Native Americans, it has been settled for barely a hundred years." During five years of active research by the Washington State Folklife Council, many people have made such comments. Native Americans have, of course, maintained their traditions here for thousands of years, but other people brought traditions with them when they came here to settle, as people still do today.

Ethnically, geographically, and occupationally, Washington is one of the most diverse states in the union. Traditions were brought in from elsewhere by our pioneers and our early immigrant settlers and they are still arriving with our newest immigrants from Asia and Latin America and with job-seekers from elsewhere in the United States. New traditions have also arisen in Washington. Many of these are the traditions of contemporary occupational groups, such as loggers, wheat ranchers, and fishermen.

In the spring of 1987, the work of a dozen Washington folk artists researched by the Washington State Folklife Council was presented at the Washington State Capital Museum in Olympia as the 1987 Governor's Invitational Art Exhibition: Folk Art of Washington State. With a major grant from the National Endowment for the Arts—Folk Arts Division, the Folklife Council was able to contract three folklorists—Harry Gammerdinger, Janet C. Gilmore, and Phyllis A. Harrison—to visit the state's many communities, both east and west of the Cascades, to find a broad sample of contemporary Washington folk art for a larger, traveling exhibition in 1988. They visited hundreds of people, most of whom deserved to be included, but cost and space limited the number of final exhibitors to a mere forty-four. Ann Tippit and Nancy Worden, folk arts researchers in Seattle, were able to supply a few ethnic artists from our largest city, to add to the diversity of the exhibition. The following March, the 1988 Governor's Invitational Art Exhibition: "'For as Long as I Can Remember . . .,' The Folk Art of Washington State" opened in Olympia, later showing in Seattle, Yakima, and Spokane (1988) and Wenatchee, Anacortes, and Ephrata (1989).

Folk Arts of Washington State is a direct outgrowth of the 1987 and 1988 exhibits, funded by a Washington State Centennial Commission "Projects of Statewide Significance" grant. It is by no means the last word on the subject. It is, in fact, more of a preliminary inquiry. An exhaustive study would be far longer. Limitations of time and cost prevented researchers from visiting many localities, and there are doubtless hundreds of folk artists in Washington yet unknown outside of their own families and communities.

The authors of the four essays have attempted, first of all, to define folk art as it exists in the context of the modern world. From our field research, we offer examples of some of the kinds of folk art that can be found in our state. Finally, we attempt to explain the motivations—personal, community, and occupational—that have led to our state's profusion of folk artists.

Many of the difficult theoretical questions regarding the nature of folk art in the past, present, and future are given short shrift, again because of limitations of time and space. Readers interested in exploring these questions further are advised to consult the Bibliography. The Bibliography also lists folk art surveys of several other states. Those for Oregon (Jones, 1980 and Siporin, 1981) and Idaho (Siporin, 1984) are especially useful for comparing the folk arts of our neighbor states with those of our own. Readers may be disappointed to find relatively little in *Folk Arts of Washington State* about Native American artists. This is simply because there are so many fine books on that subject already available, especially in regard to Coastal peoples. Again, perusal of the Bibliography will prove useful to the reader interested in learning more about Washington's Indian artists and craftspeople. Although storytelling, poetry, music, and dance are briefly discussed in the text, they cannot be adequately represented therein. These arts are by nature performance-oriented, and come to life only in the context of interaction between performer and audience. Our research has mainly been in the area of visual arts and this book is thus primarily a survey of material folk art in Washington State. Readers are encouraged to attend festivals listed in the Ethnic Resource Guide in order to enjoy the talents of Washington's folk artists who specialize in performance. At such festivals, one will also encounter craftspeople, sometimes selling, demonstrating, or exhibiting. Readers who wish to do a little research on these artists may start by attending some of these events.

The artists featured in *Folk Arts of Washington State* are among our state's living treasures, as are many individuals we were not able to visit because of cost and time limitations. The work of researching and presenting the folk arts of our state has only just begun. It is appropriate that in our Centennial year, we should offer a look at some of this material. We do so with the hope that people throughout the state will honor and appreciate the folk artists in their communities. We also hope that museums, libraries, schools, cultural institutions, and individuals will discover more artists, celebrate their talents, and present them to the public. ❖

ACKNOWLEDGMENTS

Folk Arts of Washington State is the work of many individuals and organizations. Major funding for research was provided by the National Endowment for the Arts—Folk Arts Division, the Washington State Arts Commission—Partnership Award Program, and the Washington State Centennial Commission's "Projects of Statewide Significance" Program. Additional funding came from the Littlefield Foundation (thanks to Ed and Caroline Littlefield), the Washington Commission for the Humanities, the John W. and Clara C. Higgins Foundation (thanks to Lisa Higgins Null), and the Washington State Capital Museum Foundation.

The long-term vision for a statewide folk arts project came from Michael Croman, Executive Director of the Washington State Arts Commission. Without his encouragement and support, none of this work would have been possible. Mr. Croman, Karen Gose, Director of the Commission's Partnership Awards Program, and all of the State Arts Commissioners are directly responsible for financial support of the Folklife Council through ongoing Partnership Awards, as is the staff and the Review Panel of the National Endowment for the Arts—Folk Arts Division. Financial support for the Council's establishment was due in part to the work of Margot Knight, former Assistant Director of the Washington Commission for the Humanities.

The work of the Washington State Folklife Council has been helped in great measure by the support and cooperation of the Office of the Secretary of State and the State Archives. Thanks to Hon. Ralph Munro, Secretary of State (and Centennial Commission Co-Chair), and Sid McAlpine, State Archivist.

Research for this book also led to the development of two major statewide folk art exhibitions. The first of these was the 1987 Governor's Invitational Art Exhibition: Folk Art of Washington State, at the Washington State Capital Museum in Olympia, curated by Lisa Hill-Festa. The second exhibition was the 1988 Governor's Invitational Art Exhibition: "'For As Long As I Can Remember . . .,' The Folk Art of Washington State," curated by Susan Torntore of the Washington State Capital Museum. The latter exhibit was shown in 1988 at the Washington State Capital Museum in Olympia, the Northwest Folklife Festival at the Seattle Center, the Yakima Valley Museum and Historical Society in Yakima, and the Museum of Native American Cultures in Spokane, and in 1989 at the North Central

Washington Museum in Wenatchee, the Anacortes Museum, and the Grant County Historical Society Museum in Ephrata. Portions of the exhibit were shown in the Legislative Building and the Olympia Community Center.

The exhibitions were juried by selection committees consisting of the following individuals: 1987—Patsy Callaghan, D.A.; Scott Nagel; Constance Walton, A.S.A.; Virginia White. 1988—Scott Nagel; Constance Walton; Virginia White; Nancy Worden.

Governor Booth Gardner of the State of Washington presented the 1988 Governor's Award of Commendation to Sauk Indian basketmaker Edith Bedal of Darrington and the late Richard Carl Peterson, carver, of Ephrata, "for their long-standing personal efforts to nourish the traditions of their work, to keep them vital and strong by sharing their skills and visions with others."

The statewide folk art exhibitions were originally conceived by the staff of the Washington State Capital Museum: Derek Valley, Director; David Nicandri, Chief Curator; and Lisa Hill-Festa, Curator of Exhibits.

The excellent studio photographs of artifacts from the exhibition, "'For as Long as I Can Remember . . .,' The Folk Art of Washington State," which are included in this volume, were made by photographer Teresa Manry of Wenatchee, with the cooperation of the staff of the North Central Washington Museum. Other photos are by Harry Gammerdinger, Janet C. Gilmore, Phyllis A. Harrison, Jens Lund, Steven Ohrn, and Ann Tippit. The map of Washington was drawn by Randal Hunting.

The Washington State Folklife Council wishes to thank the following individuals for helping to make this project possible:

First, thanks to all of the artists who were interviewed by Folklife Council staff and contract researchers since 1984. The hospitality and cooperation of the excellent folk artists and performers of Washington State have been key factors in the success of this project. Although space permitted only twelve artists to be included in the 1987 exhibit and only forty-four in 1988-89, several hundred artists were actually interviewed and most were deserving of inclusion. Thanks also to the artists whose works appear in this book for permission to print these photos.

The following artists and artists' family members were interviewed:

Luke Benner, Ruth Benner, Lucile Clinkenbeard, Marie Bakke Bremner, Alfredo Campos, John Engfer, Doug Harrison, Elsie Koehler Johnson, Jeffrey Melcher, Rodney Melcher, John Gross, Otto Oja, Betty Roberts, Lloyd Roberts, George Swanaset, Maria Wirkkala, Oiva Wirkkala, Cecilia Abrahamson, Edith Bedal, Dean Curtis, R.J. Burrows, Yang Mee Xiong, Chia Thao, See Xiong, Vada S. Colvin, Lida Demus, Clarence DeWitt, Andrew J. Evich, George Flett, Monad Graves, Dawn Grytness, Carl Guhlke, Thorleif (Tom) Hageland, K.E. Hartbauer, Emile Sigurd Indrebo, Petra Jiménez, John Kornyk, Theodore (Tete) Lugnet, Fred Marquand, Pete Merrill, Faye Morris, Don Olson, Karol Osusky, Kimi Ota, Dorothy Wooldridge Person, Richard Carl Peterson, Otto Franz Stieber, Frank Swalander, Woodrow Gifford, Hazel Underwood, Ada Whitmore, Bette Yamamoto, Elisabeth Krom, Hazel Behar, Cal Swan, Alfred Berndt, Lyle Bland, Diana Blines, Walter (Buzz) Culbert, Lydia Dammann, Marian Dammann, Steve Darwood, Monty Day, Sally DeWitt, Maria Diaz, Blanche Dubois, Deane Duvall, Jack Sexton, Gary Eagle, Mildred Edgemon, Paul Feddersen, Debbie Finley-Justus, Tedi Fletcher, Clint Goodwin, Dave Goodwin, Cesaria Gracia, Grace Hansen, Wilbur Harlan, Barbara Hines, June Huntzinger, Greg Colfax,

Jay B. Jurgensen, Diane Kenner, Hazel Kikendall, Leonard Kuhlmann, Bill Long, Mike Lynch, Robert Chamberlain, Bruce Morrison, Ravadi Quinn, Betty Raymer, Nancy Raymond, Bob Ren, Lorena Seelatsee, Delsie Selam, Sylvia Schaedel, Michael Schaefer, Modesta Shadle, Lisa Silvan, Judd Smith, Jacob Stappler, Jim Stone, Mrs. James Teel, John Thomsen, Kenneth Toop, Tom Tugaw, Geneva Wallace, Peggy Watson, Orval Wallace, Clark Whitmore, Goldie LeSamiz, Mee Yang Xiong, Benita Zamaripa, Sharon Zanca, Ida Hempel, Dena Johnston, Clara Post, Blanche Maberry, Riekus Duim, Vivian Margaritis, Betty Russell, Hazel Montague, Blanche Manchester, Fred Bulmer, Enola Gillaspie, Christine Coffman, Don Bray, William Krager, Ruby Brueckner, Viola Salme Ullakko, Helen Crenshaw, Nancy Larson, Viola Koski Wirkkala, Maarit Kattilakoski, Hazel Underwood, Ethel Fox, Florence Buck, Solveig Indrebo, Linda Estes, O.C. Helton, Joe (Coy) Brown, Charles (Chuck) Campbell, Cy Williams, Terry Williams, Lorraine Hutch, Hazel Holm, Shannon Pablo, Kathy Peterson, Sylvia Skeers, Clyde Williams, Sr., Raymond Fryberg, Sr., Louise Morgan, Christine Sonntag, Sarah Albert Quaempts, Margie Black, Branko Borozan, M.D., Al Anderson, Nora Anderson, Elene Emerson, Mina Sacho, Andy Wilbur, Charlie Yost, Richard Queen, Viola McCullough, Toni Vercillo, Linda Charlie, Josephine Mladenich, Ann O'Brien, Henry Smith, Floyd Broadbent, Everett Lynch, Bob Taylor, Diane Kenner, Joffre Dubois, Ben Bafus, Pat I. Gibson, John O. McMeekin, and Leo Dini.

Thanks also to all of the members of the Board of Directors of the Washington State Folklife Council, past and present, for volunteering their time and energy to guide the Folklife Council through its first six years of operation. They are:

Carlton Appelo, Burton J. Bard, Jr., Marjorie Bangs Bennett, Marilyn Bentz, Patsy Callaghan, Jean Coberly, Christine Conry, Ann L. Cowan, Susan Dwyer-Shick, Diane M. Ellison, Marcia Elston, Frank Ferrel, Penn Fix, Marilyn Hanna, Ellen Hofmann, Versa K'Ang, Barbara Krohn, Margaret Read MacDonald, Lynne Masland, Jeff Mauger, Bob Mull, Scott Nagel, Representative Dick Nelson, Alice B. Nugent, Janet Rasmussen, Mary Ellen Rowe, Richard D. Scheuerman, Richard Scholtz, Henning Sehmsdorf, Dell Skeels, Walt Smith, Henry-York Steiner, Bud Stewart, Cynthia Todd, Agnes Tulee, Ellen Vaughn, Marlys Swenson Waller, Susan Winegardner, and Nancy Worden.

Numerous other individuals and organizations played a part in making this project a success. The following is a partial list:

Bess Lomax Hawes, Dan Sheehy, Barry Bergey, Sealja James, Eileen Rowton, Jackie Cook, Jill Osborn, Minnie Larrew, Karen LaClair, Jim Leary, Steven Ohrn, Andy Bartels, Ann Bates, Finley Hays, Jean Hays, Bill Iund, Vi Iund, Robert E. Walls, Steve Siporin, Suzi Jones, Hal Cannon, Madilane Perry, Donna J. Bunten, Sharon Rasmussen, Nancy Patterson, Susan Auerbach, Vince Hughes, Sid White, Pat Matheny-White, Della Jakasovic, Paula Penry, Doug Barnes, Lorna Johnson, Sara L. Lund, Martin Lepore, Sam Scherer, Sherri Wenrick, Bill Shepherd, Peter Revill, Ellie Revill, Tomas Black, Mal Pena Chang, Judy Noall, Vivian T. Williams, Vance Horne, Don Duncan, Cecilia Goodenow, Bill Oliver, Lois Smith, Ron Macdonald, Ricˇardas Vidutis, Sally Cairns, Elaine Thatcher, Dennis Coelho, Carol Sword, Wilfred Woods, Barney McClure, Shirley Stewart, Geoff Haworth, Mary Goodrich, Pete Smith, Linda Laalen, Tom Brisk, Linda Erickson, Bertram Levy, M.D., Mia McEldowney, Joanie Taylor, Ed Morken, Mary Thomsen, Michael Warner, Keith Petersen, Mary Reed, Ann Tippit, Hal Cannon, Sandy Brightbill, Mickey Montgomery, Mary Louise Loe, Jakob Gross, Linda Day, Ken Hansen, Arlene Palmer, Noreen Robinson, Kent Martin, Irene Martin, Vivian Adams, Marilyn Bentson, Tim Boles, Keith Williams, Bill Wuorinen, the Cambodian Buddhist Temple of Tacoma, Lynden Pioneer Museum, Grant County Historical Society Museum, Ethnic Heritage Council of the Pacific Northwest, Lynden Community Center, Eastern Washington State Historical Society, Tim Kloberdanz, the Martha Circle of the United Congregational Church of Naselle, Samish Tribal Center, Yakima Nation Cultural Center, Ilwaco Heritage Museum, Okanogan County Museum, Stevens County Historical Society and Museum, Spokane Folklore Society, Seattle Folklore Society, Seattle Chapter of the Croatian Fraternal Union of America, Yakima Chapter of the American Historical Society of Germans From Russia, Tulalip Tribal Center, Skokomish Indian Tribe, MIA Gallery, Asotin County Historical Society, the Ethnic Heritage Committee of the Washington State Centennial Commission, Pullman Chamber of Commerce, Central Washington University English Department, University of Washington Comparative Literature Department, Woodland Logging Supply Company, the Molson Grange #1069, Arbiter Antiques Appraisers, Inc., the Northwest Folklife Festival, Tacoma Community House, the Mission Circle Quilt Group of Glad Tidings Assembly of God of Darrington, and North Central Washington Museum.

Special thanks to Scott Nagel, Henning Sehmsdorf, Marlys Swenson Waller, and Nancy Worden for their helpful comments and suggestions on the manuscript at various stages of completion, and to Scott Nagel, Jim Rosengren, and Diane Ellison for overseeing the production of the book. ❖

Map of WASHINGTON: Places Cited

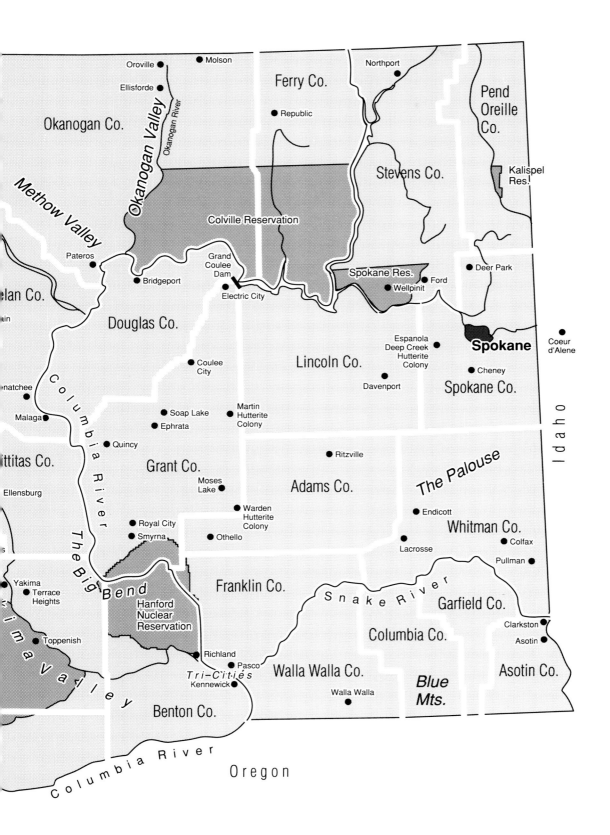

Oroville •   • Molson

Ellisforde •

Okanogan Co.

Ferry Co.

Northport •

Pend
Oreille
Co.

• Republic

Kalispel
Res.

Stevens Co.

Okanogan River

Okanogan Valley

Methow Valley

Pateros •

Colville Reservation

• Deer Park

elan Co.

Grand
Coulee
Dam

Bridgeport •

Spokane Res.

• Ford

ain

Electric City

• Wellpinit

Douglas Co.

Espanola
Deep Creek
Hutterite
Colony •

Spokane

Coeur
d'Alene •

Coulee
City •

Lincoln Co.

• Cheney

Spokane Co.

natchee
•

Davenport

Malaga •

Soap Lake •

Martin
Hutterite
Colony

Ephrata •

Quincy •

ittitas Co.

Columbia River

Grant Co.

Ritzville •

Idaho

Ellensburg

Moses
Lake

Adams Co.

The Palouse

The Big

Royal City •

Warden
Hutterite
Colony

Endicott •

Smyrna •

Othello •

Whitman Co.

Yakima
• Terrace
Heights

Bend

Lacrosse

Colfax •

Franklin Co.

Snake River

Pullman •

Hanford
Nuclear
Reservation

Garfield Co.

Toppenish •

ima Valley

Richland •

Columbia Co.

Clarkston

Tri-Cities

Pasco •

Kennewick •

Walla Walla Co.

Asotin

Blue
Mts.

Asotin Co.

Benton Co.

Walla Walla •

Columbia River

Oregon

Doug Harrison of Yakima grew up hunting and fishing with his father and grandfather near Coeur d'Alene, Idaho. Unlike most woodcarvers, Harrison is not self-taught, but learned directly from his grandfather. He specializes in miniature wildlife carvings, which he sells at craft shows, and he has taught other carvers in the Yakima Valley. Woodcarving has always been a passion of his and he was instrumental in organizing the Yakima Regional Woodcarvers' Association.

INTRODUCTION: WHAT ARE THE FOLK ARTS OF WASHINGTON STATE?

by Jens Lund

Growing up in the Idaho Panhandle near Coeur d'Alene, young Doug Harrison learned to hunt and fish from his father and grandfather. Like many older men in the North American West, his grandfather, William E. Harrison, was an adept whittler, who favored representations of local game. He taught his grandson to carve, and carving has been Doug's passion ever since—while he served in Viet Nam, while he lived in Bremerton, and since he moved to Yakima in 1983. Today Doug is in his mid-thirties, and his realistically carved and painted representations of trout, nuthatches, and eagles have been exhibited in museums all over Washington. He has also organized the Yakima Regional Woodcarvers' Association and has taught and promoted woodcarving in the Yakima area. Few would quarrel with the notion that Doug Harrison is one of our state's leading folk artists. But fewer still could define or describe what makes his work folk art, except perhaps to note that he has not been formally trained as an artist.

To understand the work of an artist like Doug Harrison, one must not only understand the idea of folk art, but also the community or communities in which it originated and in which it flourishes. The word "community," as used in folk art studies, is itself rather complex, for it refers not only to groups of individuals living in geographic proximity, but also to communities of shared identity. Shared identity may come from a common ethnic origin. It may also derive from occupation, such as logging, ranching, or teaching. Or it may even be derived from shared leisure interests, such as hunting or sports fishing. The important factor is that the community's members see themselves as having an important identifying characteristic in common.

1

Washington's Communities

Washington State has been notable for the diversity of its communities since before non-Indian settlement. Two very different Native American cultures, the Plateau and the Northwest Coastal Indians, lived and still live in the areas now enclosed within Washington's boundaries. Some Indians live on reservations, some in cities, and some in rural areas or small towns near reservations. It is difficult to agree on the exact number of tribes, but there were once scores of linguistic, cultural, and political groups on the Indian cultural landscape.

The first non-Indian settlers were fur traders, French-Canadian and French-Canadian-Indian laborers, and Scottish supervisors. The "pioneer" or "wagon train" settlers were mostly people from the Midwest, of British Isles and German ancestry. Settlers also entered Washington territory from the Willamette Valley, among them many people from the northeastern or north central states. Asians, especially Chinese, were also among our earliest non-Indian settlers. Large numbers of Scandinavians, especially Swedes, Norwegians, and Finns, settled in Western Washington at the turn of the century, working mostly as loggers and fishermen. Volga Germans from Central Russia settled most of the agricultural land of Central and southeastern Washington at that time, while immigrants from Germany concentrated in Western Washington, especially Pierce County.

During the early twentieth century, Washington received its share of the tremendous influx of immigrants into the United States from Central, Southern, and Eastern Europe. Croatian-speaking fishermen from the Dalmatian Coast (then part of Austria-Hungary, now part of Yugoslavia), Greek fishermen from the Aegean and the Sea of Marmara, Italian produce farmers, Ashkenazi Jews from Poland, Germany, Russia, and Austria-Hungary, and Sephardic Jews from Rhodes and Turkey were among the most visible of these newcomers. Western Washington also received an influx of Japanese and Dutch horticulturists in this century. Settlers from the Southwest introduced cattle ranching into arid Central Washington. After the development of irrigation in that region, Midwestern settlers arrived to develop agriculture. Mexicans from Mexico and Chicanos from the south-western states came to the irrigated valleys to work as farm laborers. Many of them subsequently settled down and gave the Yakima Valley its strong Hispanic imprint.

From the early to mid-twentieth century, several other waves of settlers from other parts of the United States came to Washington. Southeastern loggers, called "Tarheels" whether or not they hailed from North Carolina, concentrated in the eastern Skagit and Snohomish counties, and parts of Cowlitz and Lewis counties. Southeasterners, Texans, and Oklahomans were attracted by mill work in Kelso-Longview and Tacoma, and by defense industries around Puget Sound and at the Hanford works. Filipinos concentrated in both the Seattle area and the Yakima Valley. Washingtonians of

These miniature wildlife carvings are by Doug Harrison of Yakima. Such carvings are often found in communities where hunting and fishing are important leisure activities.

3

Looking at Elsie Koehler Johnson's seed-art collage-mural of the Koehler Homestead near Molson reveals the variety of materials that she uses in her artistic expression. This mural belongs to her daughter, who still lives in Molson.

Irish descent scattered across the state and tended not to concentrate in any particular location.

Following World War II, another wave of European immigrants entered, especially from areas most devastated by the war or most traumatized by post-war political realignments. Much of the state's Japanese population was lost in wartime deportations or scattered by internment, although the community has now largely recovered its numerical strength. A few Black Americans were among our earliest settlers. Groups of them arrived later, populating mining communities in the Cascades, but Blacks were never numerous here until World War II, when many came as military personnel and defense workers, mostly to Seattle, Tacoma, and the Tri-Cities.

During the past decade, Washington's population has been increased by the New Immigrants. These include Southeast Asians, many of them

Yang Mee Xiong tells the story of the Hmong people's escape from Laos during the Indochina War in an elaborate paj ntaub *or "story cloth." This relatively new form of folk art was developed in refugee camps in Thailand during the 1970s and has been a source of income for many Hmong people since their arrival in North America.*

political refugees from Cambodia, Laos, and Viet Nam. Among the Laotians are people from the Hmong and Mien mountain tribes, noted for their fine needlework. War refugees from Central America, especially El Salvador, and recent immigrants from Mexico and East Asia (including Korea, the Philippines, and Thailand) have added significantly to the state's ethnic diversity. Native Americans from other states, especially Alaska and the Plains states, and from British Columbia have made an important impact on the arts in the Seattle area. Among the more visible recent immigrants from Canada have been colonies of German-speaking Hutterites, Christian communal agriculturists from Canada's prairie provinces who have settled in colonies in Central and Eastern Washington.[1]

The complexity of Washington's ethnic mosaic is matched by its variety of occupational communities. As our nation's economy has shifted its orientation, more and more Washingtonians hold clerical, professional, and service positions. However, there are still certain occupations that have been important to the state's history and to the economy of rural communities. Such occupations have what folklorists call "high context." These are jobs that define a whole way of life not only for the worker, but also for the worker's family and community. Probably the most characteristic high context occupation in Washington is logging.[2] Washington's loggers work in the pine forests of the northeastern and north central counties and in the

Maria Wirkkala of Naselle learned to weave and spin while growing up in Finland during World War II. After moving to the United States in the 1950s, she continued weaving in the traditional Finnish styles of täkänä *and* raanu. *Her works are displayed at the Finnish-American Folk Festival in Naselle, where she often demonstrates spinning and weaving to the public.*

wet forests of the Cascades, the Olympics, and the Willapa Hills. Western Washington loggers are part of an occupational subculture that stretches from southeast Alaska to Northern California.[3]

Ranchers and their hired workers have given a significant cowboy imprint to some parts of Central Washington. They are part of a cowboy subculture that extends all the way from Mexico to Canada. The sense of danger, isolation, and camaraderie shared by loggers and by cowboys is also characteristic of Washington's fishing community, whose occupational subculture also transcends state and national boundaries.

Migrant agricultural workers are another high context occupational group that transcends political boundaries. In Washington, they were once mostly Anglo-Americans from the southwestern and south central states, who were displaced by the agricultural crisis of the 1930s. Many were also Filipinos who entered the country as U.S. Nationals when the Philippines was a U.S. Commonwealth. Today, most are Hispanic-Americans from Mexico and Central America, who also maintain a very strong ethnic identity, especially through the Spanish language.

Washington's human landscape has also been strongly affected by orchardry and wheat ranching, although people in these occupations may not have developed the intense solidarity seen among cowboys, fishermen,

Tatting, a type of knotted lace made with a shuttle, is a traditional art among women all over North America. The work of Vada Colvin of LaCrosse, Whitman County, is unusual for its third dimension. Colvin often enters her pieces in county fairs and regularly wins blue ribbons.

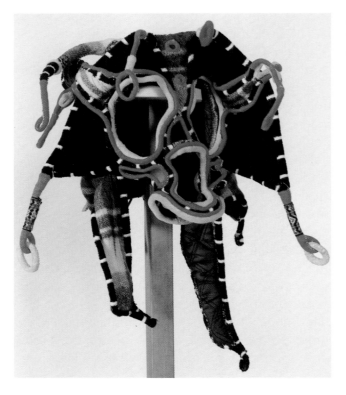

A native of Chicago, Monad Graves works with fabric and ceramics. Today he operates a health-food store on Capitol Hill in Seattle. His inspirations come from the Black communities of North America and the West Indies. The mask shown here is typical of the embroidered soft sculpture that he wears at festive and ceremonial occasions.

The Yakima Valley is home to thousands of Hispanic-Americans. Petra Jiménez of Toppenish, an immigrant from the State of Jalisco in Mexico, makes and embroiders dresses similar to the ones she once wore as a young dancer. The strikingly bright and detailed articles that she makes and decorates are worn at local fiestas in Central Washington by family members and other Mexican-Americans who purchase them from her. "I learned it all in Mexico," she says.

Lida Demus of Spokane learned needlework from her mother when she
was a child in the Ukraine. Flight
from war and occupation brought her
and her family to Germany, Argen-
tina, and ultimately to the United
States. She has studied Ukrainain
cross-stitch embroidery for years, but
first began making large wall hangings during Spokane's Expo '74.
Smaller wall hangings intended to
be hung over icons, embroidered ta-
blecloths, altar cloths, and clothing
are among the many items she makes
in the traditional Ukrainian style.

The quilts that Marie Bakke Bremner of Republic makes are original designs. She learned
needlework from her Norwegian mother, but she has also made quilts for most of her adult
life. Bremner favors pale colors, understated piecing, and elaborate stitching.

9

and loggers. People working in the aircraft, shipyard, dairy, wood-product, mining, nuclear, and transportation industries also share cultural expressions based on their work, but these expressions have not been as visible as those of high context occupations. Nonetheless, some individuals invent ways of deriving artistic expression from their professional skills. An example is the late Walter (Buzz) Culbert of Pasco, who was rated a highly skilled welder by the exacting standards of the nuclear industry. In his spare time, using skills derived directly from his profession, he created finely detailed small-scale metal sculptures, which were widely admired in the Hanford-Tri-Cities area. Culbert also taught his welding techniques to other metal workers in the area, such as Jacob Stappler, also of Pasco.

One of the most fertile sources of folk art is domestic work. In the days when most work by women was performed in the home, many of the more creative women found ways to express their artistic talents in elaborations of domestic skills. The most obvious example is the North American quilt, found all over the United States and Canada, especially, but not exclusively,

Although Dorothy Wooldridge Person of Battle Ground is best known for her fine needlework and lace, she is also an avid canner and preserver of fruit. The fruit pieces are carefully chosen for color and arranged for symmetry, making her pantry shelves aesthetically pleasing.

Faye Morris of Quincy learned to make "safety-pin-woven" rugs after seeing them in bazaars and craft shows in Central Washington. She sought out a weaver whose work she admired, Betsy Powell of Bridgeport, and Powell taught her the technique, which uses a safety pin as a shuttle. These rugs are often mistaken for braided rugs, which are superficially similar. "Safety-pin-woven" rugs are far more durable and are less likely to warp after washing.

Hazel Underwood of Taholah grew up on the Skokomish Reservation near Shelton. She learned traditional Native American basketmaking by watching her mother, despite the fact that her mother declined to teach her directly. She used to make cedar bark baskets, but has been unable to obtain a consistent supply of raw materials in recent years. Today she specializes in sewn cattail and bear-grass (raffia) baskets, which are sold to collectors.

A cedar-bark and bear-grass basket by Hazel Underwood of Taholah depicts a five-person canoe as a part of its weave. Human and animal designs are often incorporated into the design of Twana (West Puget Sound) baskets. Such work has familial and spiritual significance transcending the practicality of a basket as a utilitarian object.

in rural areas.[4] Other forms of work with fabric, such as embroidery, tatting, crocheting, lacemaking, cutwork, and sewing have been rich sources for artistic expression. Food preparation and preservation are also a source for folk art. Elaborate meals are a fixture of festivity among many ethnic groups and for many families. Women who do canning, especially competitively, as for a fair, create a more enduring form of gustatory folk art. For example, when Dorothy Wooldridge Person of Battle Ground cans fruit and vegetables, she prepares, selects, and arranges the individual items and pieces according to color, perfection of form, and symmetry. The finished glass jars are shelved, both in the fair booth and in the home pantry, to emphasize color scheme and symmetry.

The changing economies of communities in the western United States and changing migration patterns caused by economic realignment, refugee movement, and new immigration laws have all profoundly affected the ethnic and professional mosaic of Washington communities. As this situation remains in flux, so will the nature of Washington's population groups.

Washington also includes communities that are neither ethnic, occupational, nor local, but share common leisure interests. Communities of interest that foster artistic expression include Washington's old-time fiddlers, many of whom gather informally to play at the Washington Old Time Fiddlers' Association's regional or statewide conventions. Other such communities include patrons of Western-style square dance, who make their own costumes or rely on specialist dressmakers and tailors, and sports fishing enthusiasts, who tie their own flies or rely on specialists such as Dawn Grytness of Kalama or Clarence DeWitt of Richland. Some car enthusiasts also create folk art, although customized motorcycles and vans have largely replaced the customized "hot rod" of the 1950s. There are also patrons of particular types of music, such as "heavy metal" or "punk," who may affect very specific styles of clothing and hairdressing that incorporate artistic expression. Posters and fliers publicizing bands and concerts are a raw and ephemeral form of folk art, associated with urban popular music. The graffiti of youth subcultures, however objectionable when they deface private or public property, may also incorporate technically skilled manifestations of the group's aesthetics.[5]

Folk art is a function of community identity, whether it is based on ethnic, occupational, or other shared interests. Changes in community will result in changes in folk art. But folk art will continue to be the cultural product of communities of people whose shared identities generate characteristic skills, expressions, and aesthetics.

Defining Folk Art

The terms "folk art" and "folk artist" are widely used, but often ineptly defined and usually poorly understood. So, what is folk art? There are as

The flies tied by Dawn Grytness of Kalama are used primarily by southwest Washington steelhead fishermen. Grytness learned the techniques of fly-tying from her family and from another Kalama River craftsman, Blackie Tidd. "A fly must first of all catch the eye of the fisherman," says Grytness.

These flies were tied by Clarence DeWitt of Richland. He has been an avid fly-tier since he was fourteen years old, growing up in West Virginia. He is a lifelong fly-fisherman and his work is widely sold and used in Central Washington. It is a source of pride to DeWitt that he can tie a fly that looks like any bug that can be found.

John Kornyk of Vancouver, Washington was born in Tzeniv, Ukraine. As a boy, he learned woodworking at a local cabinetmaker's shop, and he has practiced decorative woodworking since childhood. Since coming to the United States after World War II, he has specialized in ethnic patterns. Wooden Easter eggs were given as toys to Ukrainian children, because of the fragility of real eggs. The patterns are the same ones seen on the traditional pysanky.

many definitions as there are definers, and the task is made more difficult by disagreements between different schools and confusions over terminology. The notion of folk art as a distinct entity is relatively new in North America. Although artifacts have been exhibited in the United States under the "folk art" rubric for over sixty years, it is only in the past two decades that we have made serious attempts at consistent definition, and there is as yet no fully agreed-upon understanding of what the term means.

One of the problems has been a predisposition to regionalize folk art: for example, some have questioned whether folk art exists at all in the American West.[6] Collectors and museums have long sought the *santos* and *bultos* of the Southwest and the art of Native Americans, but until recently, most materials in folk art exhibitions and collections have come from the East Coast or the eastern Midwest. The seminal folk art exhibitions of the

1920s through 1950s featured work from the Eastern Seaboard, usually materials dating from the Colonial period until the decade after the Civil War, during which there was presumably a "flowering" of American folk art, later extinguished by the products of industrial technology.[7] Despite all the exhibitions, however, no consistent definition of folk art prevailed, and it was usually defined in terms of what it was not. One common thread in the understanding of folk art was the notion of its having been produced by "untrained geniuses" working in isolation, inspired by a private aesthetic vision. For example, in a 1950 forum in *The Magazine Antiques*, which gave twelve scholars and collectors an opportunity to define folk art, the closest they came to a consensus was to agree that folk art was the work of people not trained in the academic tradition.[8]

During the early 1970s, the Smithsonian Institution and other museums started employing professional folklorists to locate folk art and artists for exhibitions and festivals. Folklorists were trained at several universities in a field that overlapped with cultural anthropology, literary history, and musicology. As a result, they brought to their work assumptions about what constituted "folktale," "folksong," and "folk music."[9] Their primary assumption was that those things labeled "folk" were the product of shared culture. In other words, a unique tale or song was not a folktale or folksong, except insofar as one could demonstrate the influence of group tradition on

The use of decoys to lure waterfowl is believed to be a Native American invention, but elaborately carved decoys are mostly made by European-Americans. Today, mass-produced decoys made of plastic or aluminum are far more economical and practical. Wooden decoys are still carved as art objects, especially in areas where waterfowl are plentiful. Pat I. Gibson of Ocean Park on the Long Beach Peninsula is one of the few women decoy-carvers in Washington. She is self-taught, but was inspired by the work of other carvers in the area.

it. This was, of course, categorically incompatible with the notion of folk art as the "product of an 'untrained genius,' working in isolation, inspired by a private aesthetic vision."

To date, this contradiction still stands, embodied in two camps of folk art interpreters, one espousing the criterion of "private vision," the other the criterion of "community tradition." Attempts to reconcile the two camps, such as the one that took place at the Library of Congress' 1983 conference, "The Washington Meeting on Folk Arts," have had limited success.[10] The dispute is as much political as philosophical, because the "private vision" constituency dates back to the 1920s and regards the "community tradition" group as upstarts. Despite decades of dominance by the "private vision" group, trained folklorists have attempted to make the term "folk art" consistent with other uses of the term "folk," as in "folksong" or "folktale." Moreover, both camps have inconsistencies. Folk art exhibitions by the "private vision" constituency have included examples of ethnic art from the Southwest. And folklorists have looked for obscure manifestations of community tradition in the work of visionary artists such as Simon Rodia, builder of the Watts Towers in Los Angeles.[11]

Today, definitions of folk art are further complicated by a confusion of the terms "art" and "craft." In fine art literature, distinctions between these two categories are often made on the basis of medium or technique. In folk art literature (both "private vision" and folklorist), art is often defined as

Lyle Bland of Wenatchee has been carving for as long as he can remember. Following a typical pattern among rural American men, he started as a young boy, but he has been most active since his retirement. He started making miniature decoys during the 1950s and full-sized ones during the 1970s. Bland has perfected a woodburning technique to make realistic-looking feather patterns.

Bette Yamamoto of Othello learned quilting from her mother, who grew up in Japan and Hawaii. Yamamoto's style and technique are derived from her mother's exposure to Japanese and Hawaiian needlework. She is very articulate about the differences between Asian/Pacific quilting and traditional Anglo-American quilting, noting particularly that in the former the stitches are much smaller and more consistent. Yamamoto has made about fifty quilts in her lifetime, all of which have been given to family and friends.

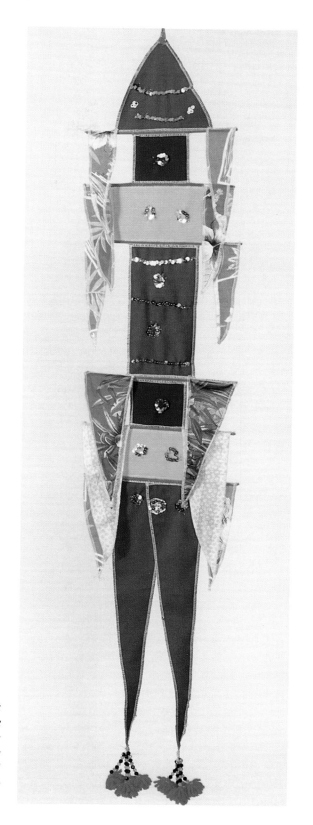

Entering the Cambodian Buddhist Temple of Tacoma, one sees the numerous tuong proleang *or "spirit flags" hanging from the ceiling. They are pieced from brightly-colored pieces of cloth and memorialize the spirits of departed loved ones.*

primarily aesthetic and craft as primarily utilitarian. In other words, paintings, carvings, and models are art, and baskets, tools, and ceramic jugs are craft. This distinction, however, is based on a limited vision, derived from the Romantic Era, in which art is categorically "pure" and free from the unwholesome taint of utilitarianism. When this distinction is accepted uncritically, it creates problems of interpretation for many artifacts. What, for example, are quilts? They keep you warm, so they are functional, and therefore craft. But they are also a principal form of aesthetic expression for North American rural women, and thus they are art. Similarly, the tradition of decorative wildfowl carving may be traceable to the production of decoys to lure waterfowl into the hunter's range. Many wildfowl carvers still carve decoys today, but few of these are used as they once were, because mass-produced plastic or aluminum decoys are cheaper and more practical. Many Native American-made artifacts have spiritual or familial functions, but non-Indians regard them as art if they are aesthetically pleasing. Objects that were once primarily utilitarian are now often made by tradition-bearers for aesthetic qualities appreciated by collectors. This is especially the case with many contemporary Native American artifacts, now made principally for sale to non-Indians. In summary, the distinction between folk art and folk craft has become so blurred that it is almost meaningless.[12] It is important to note, however, that most folk artists do not think of themselves as folk artists at all. Many of them do not even consider themselves artists. It is those who write about, study, or collect folk art who impose definitions on people who are doing what they do without self-consciousness.

The authors of the articles in this book believe that useful definitions of folk art begin with an understanding of the important role of community in the inspiration, production, and evaluation of folk art. An individual artist belongs to a specific community or group, and his or her expression is a product of that group's traditions. Such traditions can be ethnic or occupational. Or they can be shared by the people of a certain town, locality, or neighborhood, or even by the members of a particular family. Shared traditions can be skills, such as the way a member of the Tulalip tribe makes a basket or the way a Kittitas County saddler builds a saddle for working cowboys in his vicinity. More likely, the members of a community share certain aesthetic assumptions. For example, most Finns in southwest Washington are not carvers, but there is a Finnish style of carving, which Finnish-Americans appreciate. Most members of Granges in the Okanogan are not makers of seed-art collages, but the Granges of Eastern Washington have long promoted seed art, and those Grangers who have the talent are supported and appreciated when the time comes to make a display for the North Central Washington District Fair in Waterville.[13] A folk artist, therefore, works within a framework of shared traditions, aspires to express community aesthetics, and develops his or her own style and technique based on those traditions.[14] Artists in ethnic communities, such as Native

Nettie Kuneki lives on the Yakima Reservation and is descended from the Klickitat Tribe, today part of the Yakima Confederation. She comes from a long line of traditional basketmakers, and she has taught her skills to other women of the Confederation. Her baskets are made of split cedar root and bear grass and they are embellished with traditional spiritual and familial motifs. Kuneki is also the co-author of an excellent book on Klickitat basketmaking. She was recently chosen by the Burke Museum to make baskets for a special Centennial collection by outstanding Washington Indian artists.

The cornhusk bags of Sarah Albert Quaempts are of very high quality. Cornhusk bags are made by many Plateau Indian peoples. Some are used for ceremonial purposes, and today many are sold to collectors. Quaempts lives in a rural area on the Yakima Reservation and her work is sometimes on sale at the gift shop of the Yakima Nation Cultural Center in Toppenish.

"The Square Dancers" is one of the finest examples of the many carved tableaux by Richard Carl Peterson of Ephrata. More than sixty of Peterson's pieces are on display at the Grant County Historical Society Museum in Ephrata. Most are Western or pioneer scenes.

American carvers and basketmakers, Ukrainian Easter egg decorators, and Norwegian needleworkers, work within their technical and aesthetic ethnic traditions. As folk artists, they usually learned directly from informal, face-to-face contact with older members of their communities (often parents or grandparents) and their art is appreciated and evaluated by their peers. However, not all folk artists work within an ethnic tradition. For example, Doug Harrison learned to carve from his grandfather, and the subjects of his work are derived from hunting and fishing, which are popular activities in his community. Therefore, his work could be considered part of the aesthetic tradition of the community of Northwestern outdoorsmen.

It must be kept in mind that the idea of folk art is primarily Western European, based on assumptions about art and society that are not necessarily valid for non-European cultures. Consequently, when we talk about the folk art of Native Americans or Chinese-Americans (or Chinese) or Japanese-Americans (or Japanese), we risk confusing already complicated defi-

The late Fred Marquand of Bellingham grew up on the local waterfront. He was intrigued by the tattoos of the sailors he befriended, and began experimenting on himself at the tender age of twelve. During the 1920s and 1930s, he operated tattoo parlors on the Bellingham waterfront. His customers chose tattoos from watercolor templates that he painted and displayed in his shop. Marquand was also a skilled leatherworker and builder of model ships. Much of his work represents the romantic era of sail and steam navigation that fascinated him so much as a boy.

Don Schole of Vancouver, Washington is another chainsaw carver who draws his inspiration from the logging profession. A three-foot-high model of a calk shoe represents a part of the logger costume that is as characteristic and symbolic of the Northwest logger as the Stetson is of the cowboy.

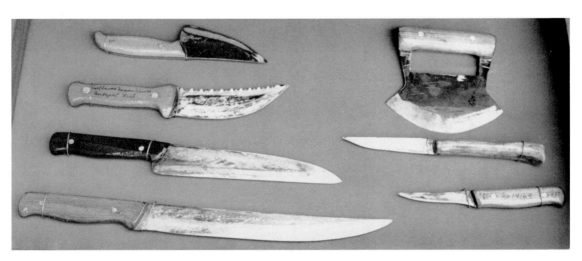

K.E. Hartbauer of Northport, in the Selkirk Range, has been designing and making knives since 1910. He also makes hammers, chisels, prybars, crowbars, and axe handles. His knives are made from old crosscut saw blades, ground carefully so as not to destroy their temper. His use of antler and bone for handles and the wide variety of shapes of his handles and blades led one collector to describe his work as "knives with soul." They are, however, working tools, intended for use by Northwest outdoorsmen. Their rough, masculine quality appeals to the hunter and sports fisherman's aesthetic.

Retired high-climber Oiva Wirkkala of Naselle was born in the United States, but he was raised speaking Finnish. "We were almost born with a pocketknife in our hands," he recalls. Although he specializes in making the kauha or Finnish wooden ladle (below), which he carves from local vine maple, Wirkkala also carves representational scenes of the logging woods in relief, and wooden door hinges, and he makes models of old log buildings.

The Norwegian Hardingfele or "Hardanger fiddle" is one of the most elaborately decorated folk instruments in the world. A close look at this example, made by the late Emile S. Indrebo of Tacoma, reveals the four resonating strings that pass through the neck and sound sympathetically when the four main strings are played.

Quirts and belts hitched by Alfredo Campos of Federal Way are made with dyed horsehair purchased from a rendering plant. Campos learned to work with rawhide while growing up on a ranch near Tucson, Arizona. He later taught himself horsehair hitching.

nitions. Regarding Native Americans, for example, the notion of art as an activity separate from social functions is inappropriate in the context of traditional Indian life. Yet today, many Native Americans are professional artists, whose work satisfies the demands of non-Indian buyers.

In both China and Japan, there are centuries-old fine arts traditions, some of which are practiced widely. Washingtonians of Chinese or Japanese origin or ancestry may practice these skills, but they are usually taught in a formal setting. Thus their work can certainly be considered ethnic art, but probably not folk art. An exception might be the *Sashiko* quilting of Kimi Ota of Seattle. Ota is an American-born needleworker who has spent significant portions of her life in Japan. *Sashiko* stitching was a family tradition. She was also influenced by American quilting, which she studied for years.[15] Needle-

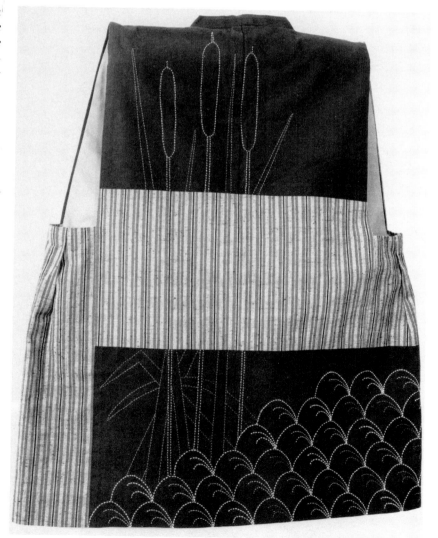

Seattle-born Kimi Ota was raised in Japan and moved back to Seattle during her adolescence. Although she learned to quilt in an adult education class, she remembered seeing Sashiko *quilting in Japan. About fifteen years ago, she returned to Japan to research the subject in depth, finding that it was nearly extinct there. She has since written a book on the technique and has taught it to others in the Japanese-American community. Pictured is the back of an embroidered and* Sashiko-*quilted* hanten *jacket.*

work of Southeast Asian mountain people, such as the Hmong and Mien, is learned informally, usually as part of a family tradition, and is thus considered folk art.

There are also folk artistic expressions that cut across group boundaries. Quilting is one of these, although it has traditionally been the work of women in small towns and rural areas. In the section of this introduction on folk media, several media appear which may not be associated with particular ethnic or occupational groups, including carving (by non-Indians),

Washington's Granges promote the making of collages from seeds and other plant material for display at county and regional fairs. Elsie Koehler Johnson of Molson (now living in Republic) may be the most imaginative "seed artist" in the state. Her collage-murals, which depict agriculture, farmsteads, and scenery in northeastern Okanogan County, are on display at the Molson Grange. Most remarkable of her works is a three-dimensional, full-sized representation of an eagle (at left), made of cedar scales with a wire frame. The eagle and most of her murals are on permanent display at the Molson Grange.

28

model-building, fabrication of miniature windmills, and "yard art." Further study may show, however, that particular manifestations of these arts may have ethnic, occupational, familial, or regional origins, and there is no doubt that some specific examples are ethnically or occupationally influenced, such as Japanese-Hawaiian quilting or logger yard art.

Folk art research consists of visiting, interviewing, and observing individuals. From such limited interactions, one can make certain generalizations, but one must treat them with caution. For example, this discussion began with an assertion about the importance of community. One paradox of folk art research is that although folk art reflects the shared aesthetics and techniques of groups of people, folk artists themselves are often very individualistic. In fact, all art (including fine art) is the product of tension between tradition and innovation. The most creative artists are able to stretch tradition, making something new that is, nonetheless, not a complete departure from tradition.

It is also wise to avoid the generalizations sometimes found in literature about folk art. Writers have asserted that this or that medium is "the only truly authentic American folk art," an assertion that is dependent on what is meant by "authentic" or "American." Another common generality is that "folk art is rapidly dying out," an assertion based on the notion that folk art is a survival of a rapidly disappearing culture, or that all folk artists are older people.[16] It is true that folk art is often made by older people, because they have both the leisure and the skills to pursue it. But that does not mean that when these particular individuals pass away their skills will become extinct. Just as people die every day, people retire every day, and among the new retirees are people with traditional skills who now have time to devote to artistic expression.

Folk artists share the traditions of their ethnic, occupational, local, or family groups, but their responses to these traditions vary. An artist may keep within the confines of a tradition, experiment with it, or combine different traditions, techniques, and skills. For example, Marie Bakke Bremner of Republic learned needlework from her Norwegian immigrant mother, and she is an accomplished stitcher of *Hardangersøm*. But she also quilts, and her quilting and piecing designs are entirely her own. Alfredo Campos of Federal Way learned traditional rawhide braiding as a boy on a ranch near Tucson, Arizona, but he has adapted this skill to develop an elaborate style of polychrome horsehair hitching. Betty Roberts of Oroville learned woodworking from her father, flower preservation from her neighbors, and spinning and weaving from living in an area where sheep are raised. She has combined these skills in her elaborate, flower-inlaid spinning wheels, which she fabricates with the help of her husband, Lloyd. The seed-art collage-murals of Elsie Koehler Johnson of Molson, Okanogan County represent an expansion of the seed art promoted by the Granges.[17]

There are also self-taught artists such as former logger Don Schole of

Vancouver, Washington, who carves with a chainsaw, and Rod and Jeff Melcher, a wheat rancher's sons from western Adams County, who create wooden models of combines, harrows, and tractors. Even though these artists acquired skills and techniques on their own, their work is appreciated by members of their respective occupational communities. Schole's carvings, which often represent woods-related themes such as beavers and calk shoes, are purchased by logging supply businesses and logging companies, and displayed in their shops or offices. The Melcher brothers' models find their way into the homes of wheat ranchers, the offices of implement dealers, and booths at Central Washington fairs.

Although Marie Bakke Bremner of Republic is best known in Ferry County for her quilts, she has practiced the Norwegian folk art of Hardangersøm *since childhood, having learned it from her mother, who was a Norwegian immigrant. The technique, which is a form of counted-thread cutwork, probably has its origins in the ancient Middle East, but work of this type spread throughout Europe during the Renaissance. Its highest expression in Northern Europe took place in the Norwegian district of Hardanger, which was also a source of many Norwegian immigrants to the United States. Today, many Norwegian-American women practice the skill as an artistic expression of ethnic identity.*

Folk Art Media In Washington

Just as Washington enjoys a tremendous ethnic diversity, there is also a diversity of different expressions of folk art—two-and three-dimensional, representational, and abstract, using wood, metal, fabric, or thread. The writers of this book encountered many manifestations or media of Washington folk art during their research. Their research was in no way exhaustive, but the results of the past four years have yielded much suggestive data. This data includes information not only on the media, but also on the

Among Washington's most innovative folk artists are Betty and Lloyd Roberts of Oroville. Betty Roberts learned lathe-turning and cabinet-making from her father, spinning and weaving and the drying of flowers from neighbors in the Okanogan Valley. She has combined these skills to produce a unique line of finely-engineered spinning wheels, inlaid with epoxy-mounted dried flowers and butterflies. Her husband, Lloyd, designs and machines the metal parts. Betty and Lloyd Roberts' spinning wheels are marketed all over North America.

relationship between the medium and such factors as ethnicity, occupation, region, physical environment, age group, and influences outside the community.

Folk art media in Washington reflect the skills and interests of folk communities. One distinctive Northwestern occupational folk art is logger genre painting. Genre painting has been an important artistic form for professional and amateur painters since the Romantic period. Genre painting is often highly localized, and frequently portrays landscapes. In Washington, mountain, seacoast, and forest scenes are common subjects, as are depictions of wildlife, particularly game. Local economies also influence genre painting, so one is likely to find wheat ranch paintings in the Palouse, cattle ranch paintings in Ellensburg (site of the Annual Western Art Show

The image of the logger may appear in the domestic arts of logging families. The late Laura Wuorinen of Naselle made apple-head dolls that were unmistakably loggers—note the calk shoes and tin hat. This doll was on display at the 1986 Finnish-American Folk Festival in Naselle.

and Auction), and seascapes on the Long Beach peninsula. Logger genre painting is usually nostalgic, recalling the days of axes and crosscut saws and yarding by oxteams or steam donkey. Two of Washington's leading logger genre painters are Don Olson of Tacoma and Robert Chamberlain of Shelton, both of whom worked in the days before the chainsaw and the diesel yarding engine.

Although fruit box labels are often displayed in Central and Eastern Washington as a local manifestation of folk art, they are not really folk art at all, but rather a form of commercial art associated with a particular group (fruit ranchers) and therefore not directly applicable to this discussion.[18]

Some media of folk art also cross group boundaries. Carving may be associated with ethnic groups, such as Finns or Northwest Coastal Indians, or shared interest groups, such as outdoors enthusiasts or duck hunters. Most, but not all, carvers are men, and these artists are more numerous in rural or small town settings than in big cities. In much of rural North America there is a temporal pattern to woodcarving: a boy is given a knife as a rite of passage; if he has the interest and talent, he may whittle, or carve

The late Bill Swan of Asotin had a national reputation as a carver of Western caricatures. He was best known for designing the horse figure used on the Ford Mustang. A large collection of his carvings and tableaux is on display at the Asotin County Historical Society Museum.

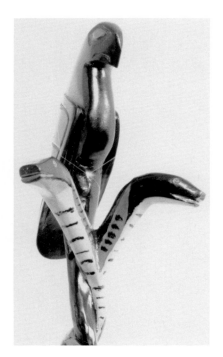

George Swanaset, an accomplished woodcarver, is a member of the Nooksack Tribe. He lives in the Native American community of Sochanon in Whatcom County and works for Intalco Aluminum of Ferndale. Swanaset is largely self-taught, but also inspired by other Indian people, whose work he has studied. He has an international reputation for his cedar racing canoes, many of which are used by Vancouver Island and American tribes in canoe races at Coastal Indian festivals. He also carves one-twelfth-scale models of racing canoes and other Native American artworks, including Salishan masks and "talking staffs," which are used to denote authority by the speaker who holds one.

small objects casually. He may be self-taught or tutored by an older relative. His interest often fades as he becomes socially acculturated during adolescence, and it may remain dormant during the professionally productive years of life, when "mere whittling" is considered loafing. After retirement, interest resumes, and he becomes a serious carver.[19] This pattern is most common in agricultural areas. It has, however, been altered somewhat by the wage-earner's eight-hour day and the post-World War II acceptance of the value of leisure activity.

Carving is usually performed on a small scale. The pocket-knife is the principal tool. Some carvers also use special knives and gouges. People in the Northwest have developed a larger form of carving, using the chainsaw. This tool first came into widespread use in Northwestern forests around 1940. Some loggers amused themselves in the woods by carving stumps into chairs and other likenesses. Chainsaw carver Otto Oja of Cathlamet saw his first chainsaw sculpture in Oregon in the early 1960s. Chainsaw sculpture

Greg Colfax of the Makah Nation finishes off a large welcoming figure for The Evergreen State College. Monumental art in public places in Washington is often carved on commission by traditional Native American artists.

Adam Benner of Endicott was born in the German-speaking community of Yagoda, in Central Russia, and moved to the Palouse in 1904. Before he passed away in 1948, Benner produced numerous elaborate, original pieces of furniture. Many of them, such as those in the photo, incorporated elaborate parquetry. The finest example is an 8,000-piece cedar chest now owned by his son, Luke, who lives in Spokane. Luke Benner remembers, "[His children] didn't think he had much patience, but he did have it with that kind of work." (Photo courtesy of Luke Benner.)

is now common in forested areas of North America. Some Western Washington timber towns, such as Aberdeen and Raymond, display large monuments chainsaw-carved from old growth logs. Today, most Native American carvers who work with wood on a large scale rough out the large pieces, such as welcoming figures and totem poles, with a chainsaw.[20]

The totem pole is an icon of the Northwest landscape. It is, however, not really indigenous to Washington but rather to the British Columbia coast and southeast Alaska. Some of Washington's Coastal peoples have adopted them in recent years, and examples can be seen at tribal headquarters of the Puyallup, Quileute, Suquamish, and Tulalip, and in a historical Makah burial place. Most of the monumental totem poles in public parks were carved by Indians from farther north, or by non-Indians. In fact, there are probably more bogus totem poles carved by non-Indians in Washington

Karol Osusky of Seattle comes from an unbroken line of Slovakian cabinetmakers and woodworkers going back to the sixteenth century. He is an immigrant from Czechoslovakia and learned woodworking from his father. Osusky specializes in Slovakian peasant furniture and also makes wayside crosses, such as the one shown here. These crosses were traditionally used in Eastern Europe to mark property and parish boundaries. One of his crosses is on display at the Union Gospel Mission in Seattle's Pioneer Square.

than genuine items. This is due to the totem pole's status as a regional symbol, reinforced by its widespread use in advertising and trademarks.

Carving also figures in the creation of models. Model-building has a typical pattern, comparable to small-scale carving. Many model-builders are retired people who were skilled tradesmen during their years of employment, and their models may be inspired by local themes. In rural areas, one finds farmstead or ranch tableaux; near the coast, ship or boat models are common. In Washington's logging communities, we find models of logging operations, usually from the romanticized oxen or steam eras.

Cabinetmaking is an important folk art in many communities. In Western Washington, traditional cabinetmakers are often Scandinavian, and in Eastern Washington many are of Volga German origin. Among the Hutterites, each colony has a master cabinetmaker, who not only makes items for use within the colony, but also for sale to the outside world.

Other examples of folk art are found in "yard art" or "folk art environments": birdhouses, rock gardens, scarecrows, decorative mailbox posts, flower gardens, and more ephemeral forms, such as snowmen and sand castles. These expressions may be influenced by participation in a group aesthetic. There are examples of logger yard art in many wooded parts of Washington. These are usually pieces of choker cable or blocks or stumps

Travelers along the Olympic Highway who pass through Central Park can hardly help noticing the grotto-like yard art assemblage in the front yard of John O. McMeekin. A retired logger who still works in the timber industry as a safety consultant, McMeekin has been collecting old logging equipment for years. His yard assemblage is unique, but he is often called upon to decorate booths at logging equipment shows, which he does by lending some of the more movable pieces from his collection.

with springboard holes used to line driveways or support mailboxes. Retired logger John O. McMeekin of Central Park, near Aberdeen, has assembled a huge collection of old logging equipment into a fantasy landscape. McMeekin was recently asked to design display booths at logging equipment exhibitions.[21] Finnish-American carver Oiva Wirkkala of Naselle builds birdhouses that resemble Finnish log cabins. Carvers and woodworkers also produce model windmills called whirligigs, also called "mole chasers," because their vibrations supposedly annoy moles and discourage their burrowing. Yard art is also created by elaborate rhododendron and azalea plantings, usually found in middle class neighborhoods of Puget Sound's cities and suburbs. In Spokane, profuse plantings of lilacs are a typical landscaping feature.

The Intangible Folk Arts

Folk art is usually regarded as material culture, consisting of artifacts. But equally important are the intangible arts, such as storytelling, music, and dance. The Washington State Folklife Council has not yet researched these areas with any degree of thoroughness, so it would be presumptuous of us to attempt to describe their manifestations in Washington. It is important for us to point out, however, that these expressions are as much a form of folk art as any of the material culture discussed and depicted in this book. Washington has a rich store of traditional narration, song, dance, and instrumental music that has yet to be researched in any kind of depth.

Because the aesthetic dimension of telling a tale is often of great significance, the art of storytelling tends to persist even in many literate cultures. The informality of narration in modern settings, however, prevents recognition of storytellers outside their informal groups: office ranconteurs and tavern tale-tellers are not accorded the recognition given to quilters and carvers, however much they may be heroes at the workplace or neighborhood bar.

Among Washington's Native Americans, storytelling is an important feature of cultural revitalization. Tribal elders have used traditional tales to transmit their culture's beliefs and values to the younger generation, whose culture is diluted and threatened by mainstream popular culture. Some of these storytellers have achieved a degree of recognition outside their own tribal communities. Pan-Indian events, such as powwows, as well as educational forums where non-Indians are present, often feature storytellers as presenters of Native American culture.

Non-Indian ethnic communities may also have master storytellers, although they may not be regarded as such. They may be historical and genealogical researchers who are conversant with a group's history, beliefs, traditions, and customs, and who have collected family stories and anec-

Pete Merrill of Belfair is a master at making whimsical, pictorial windmills, known as "whirligigs" or "mole chasers." Such pieces are a typical homemade outdoor decoration in many parts of North America, and have even been mass-produced in recent years. Merrill's whirligigs incorporate a high degree of woodworking craftsmanship, artistic vision, and humor.

For years, the late Emil Gehrke worked for the Bonneville Power Administration at Grand Coulee Dam. During much of his life, he assembled found objects, including teapots, coffee cups, hardhats, funnels, and the like into humorous miniature windmills, which he designed himself. Today, many of Gehrke's whirligigs are displayed in a B.P.A.-owned park in Electric City, near the dam. Others are owned by Puget Sound Power and Light Company, which displays some of them at a transformer substation in Seattle.

dotes about immigration. Many are excellent narrators, both in public and private situations, and are highly regarded within their communities—but as historians, ethnic activists, or genealogists, not as storytellers.[22]

Loggers, fishermen, cowboys, and truckers are among the occupational groups that use storytelling to cement group solidarity. Such storytelling often occurs in informal settings, and is usually humorous, often exaggerated to the proportions of a tall tale. Logger publishers Finley and Jean Hays of Marys Corner in Lewis County have collected and published examples of these stories and jokes in their monthly newspaper *Loggers World* and in several books.[23]

One form of folk narrative that has been tenacious in the Northwest is occupational poetry, particularly among cowboys and loggers. Both trades have a tradition of recitation that can be traced back to the nineteenth century. Until recently, both groups communicated their poetry orally. Today, most poems appear first in ephemeral publications or in the pages of industry newspapers.[24]

Singing is still a strong tradition in many of Washington's ethnic

"The Hooker and His Lady"

by Woodrow Gifford
(Copyright 1978. Used with the author's permission.)

Woodrow Gifford is a retired logger who lives in Seaview, Washington. He is often called upon to recite his ballad-like poems at local festivals and banquets. "The Hooker and His Lady" ("hooker" or "hooktender" refers to the boss of a rigging crew) recalls a true incident of danger and tragedy, as many logger poems do.

'Twas in the High Lead Days of the Twenties
On the Blue Ridge Loggin' Show,
The Rigger was pushin' the outfit
Cause The Hooker was takin' a blow,
Down in the Resort City
Just to get away from The Show—
He would be back in a fortnight
All fired up and ready to go.

We heard The Shay a comin'
Up the windin' incline—
Then she wheezed and hissed past the Cookhouse
And stopped by the big Sugar Pine;
You could see Big Dan, The Hooker
His broad shoulders filling the door,
Quickly he stepped down to the crosswalk
Between the track and the camp warehouse door.

Big Dan sorta hesitated—
And his face seemed kinda red
Then down stepped a well dressed lady
With a wide brimmed hat on her head;
The boys glanced 'round at each other—
But nary a word was said;
We knew too well if we had of
Big Dan woulda smote us dead.

He sorta ignored us fellers
And The Lady took his arm—
She was sure in the safest of keepin'
Immune from danger and harm;
They took the board walk towards the river,
Up to The Hooker's Shack—
The Shay whistled twice for The Crossin'
and slowly chugged down the track.

Now the Camp Folks conjectured and whispered
Passin' judgement upon The Pair,

It seemed to me that the gossip
Was too soon and sorta unfair;
They said that Big Dan was a Patron
of houses displaying red lights
Where men folk were ever welcome
Anytime of the day or nite.

Big Dan was on deck the next morning
Pushin' The Sugar Pine Side
Carryin' on as usual
And takin' his work in stride;
That night when the mulligan halted
In front of the long gray cook shack—
Big Dan grabbed hold of his nose-bag
And headed across the track
A'strictly mindin' his business
And not once a lookin' back.

We noticed a strange transformation
Takin' place 'round The Hooker's Shack,
Between the stumps was fresh spaded
And the Wood Pile was moved to the back;
The windows soon lost their fly specks
White curtains were neatly tied back—
New blinds were drawn to keep out the sun
Replacin' the torn Sugar Sack.

It sure seemed a Cozy Cottage
With rocks neatly placed around,
White washed and shining like silver
When the dew was on the ground;
The Camp Folks began to notice
That progress was takin' place—
They wondered about The Lady
But she gentle like kept her place,
Shyly avoidin' her neighbors
And seldom showin' her face.

When Payday came 'round at the Campsite
The Boys had a Poker Game planned
So they approached Big Dan at the Office Gate
To come and sit in a Hand;
"No thanks," said Big Dan quickly
Never slowin' his gait
"The Lady is waitin' supper—and
I'm goin',—so's I won't be late."

Camp Life was gettin' 'bout normal
On The Blue Ridge Loggin' Show,
The logs were comin' in steady
And the Drifters would come and go—
Headin' South to the Redwoods
Before the late fall snow.

One morning in late October
They were layin' out a new road,
The Punk had whistled to clear The Lines
Before they'd bring in a load;
Big Dan was down in the Creek Bed
Makin' his way out past the line—
When an upended log came crashin' down
And hit him in the spine;
The Riggin' Slinger had just turned 'round
And saw what had happened to Dan
Quickly he whistled The Yardin' Crew in
Down they came—every last loggin' man.

'Twas a saddenin' sight to see Big Dan
In there with his broken back
He'd grasp The Huckle Brush with his hands,
And struggle,—and then lie back;
The boys looked on with tears in their eyes
While they waited The Stretcher Crew—
Dan never screamed or moaned in pain
Though his face was blotched and blue.
The Camp Rod came a'rushin' down—
And knelt close by Dan's side,
He and Dan had long been friends—
Friends that were true and tried;
"I wanna see The Lady," whispered Dan as he
    gasped for breath
He was fightin' for time, That Hooker, bravely
    holdin' off death.

We eased him onto the stretcher
Handlin' him gentle like,
Big Dan grasped hold of the side rails
and squeezed them ever so tight;
We thought he would die any minute
But he sure put up a fight.
The Camp Rod took off like a bullet
We could guess where he had gone—
To get The Hooker's Lady
Before his soul passed on.

Well, The Boys kept pushin' upward
Over the Wind Felled Trees
'Till they reached the grade of the roadbed
Then they slumped and sagged to their knees;
The Rod was comin' fast like
With The Lady by his side—
Her face white as death itself
And her eyes were set and wide.

Big Dan was sorta driftin' off
But he sensed The Lady was near,
He opened his eyes as she stifled a sob
Then held him fond and dear;
Dan faintly smiled,—then tried to speak
But his words we could not hear
The end was closin' in and fast
Thank God The Lady was near.

She seemed to freeze in that last embrace
Clutching him close to her breast,
So softly she spoke and kissed his brow
Then laid him back to rest.
Well, The Lady bowed her head—then rose
Her face so white and drawn
It seemed that not only Dan had left,
But The Lady, too, was gone.

True Marriage is made in heaven
So the Biblical Pedagogues say
I couldn't adjudge the union
Of woman and man this way,
However, by seein' The Lady
And knowin' the merits of Dan
Me-thinks they had found "the blessin'"
That true bond between woman and man.

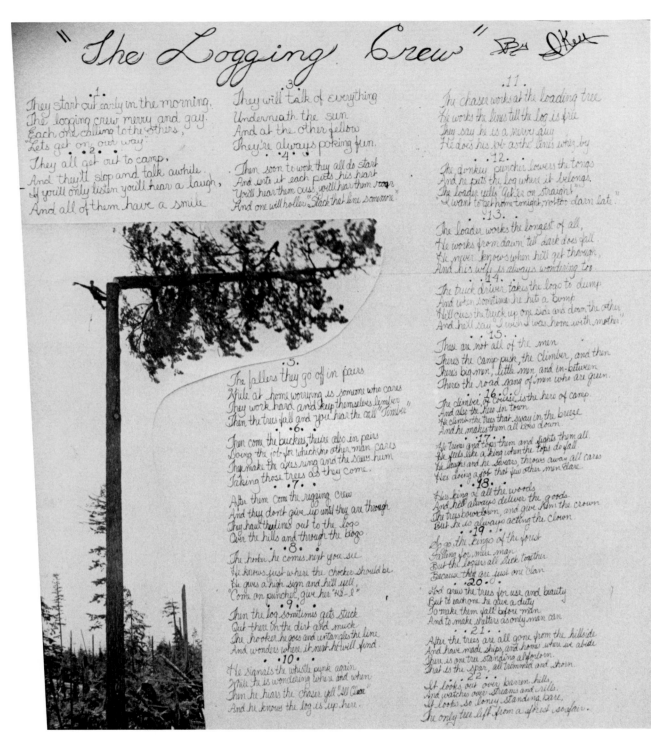

The late Ikey Wirkkala of Naselle wrote the poem "The Logging Crew" in honor of her husband, Oiva. She decorated it with a photo of him topping a tree. The collage is always displayed at the biennial Finnish-American Folk Festival in Naselle. (Photo courtesy of Oiva Wirkkala.)

communities. Traditional singing and musical ensembles in Washington flourish among many ethnic groups. However, most traditional singing by individuals occurs entirely within the home. Public and group singing and instrumental music are most visible among immigrant groups that maintain strong ethnic identity, or among Washingtonians who still strongly identify with their place of origin, whether in the United States or abroad.[25]

In Northwest Indian communities, most songs are property, and they cannot be sung without authorization from the family that owns the song. Public singing often takes place at powwows, especially when playing *slahal* or "bone games," or at potlatches. [26]

Folk Art In Modern Society

The persistence of folk art in an urban technological society may seem anomalous. There are, however, certain factors that encourage it to survive, and in some cases to flourish. Some instances of folk art survive from an era of simpler technology, such as traditional baskets woven by John Engfer of Orting. The skill is maintained because people find the baskets attractive and therefore buy them. But Engfer's baskets are also an enshrinement of preindustrial technology and a romanticization of the homemade product.

Although we may see mass communication as a homogenizing force in society, it also encourages an opposing trend, a kind of "tribalization" through long-distance communication and ease of travel. What this means is that individuals who in earlier generations would have had contact only with people in geographic proximity can now form bonds of common interest with others all over the map. For instance, Finnish-Americans in Aberdeen or Italian-Americans in Walla Walla are no longer merely part of a community of Finns or Italians in their immediate neighborhoods. They can attend meetings and communicate by mail or telephone with people at great distance. It is now possible to speak of a Finnish community in Washington as a whole, or in the Northwest, or in the entire United States. This also holds for occupational communities. Washington fishermen on the Lower Columbia are now part of a larger community of Washington fishermen along the Pacific Coast, the Strait of Juan de Fuca, Puget Sound, and the Alaskan coast. They are, of course, also part of larger communities of West Coast and American fishermen. And finally, the same trend can be found in communities of shared interests, such as wildlife carvers. Floyd Broadbent of Naches is in contact with wildlife carvers all over the Northwest, in the eastern United States, and Canada.

Folk art can be a tool for cultural revitalization. Much Native American artistic expression was annihilated during the period when Indian children were sent to boarding schools or taught by religious missionaries. The effort to make Native Americans into "mainstream Americans" produced a whole generation in which carvers, basketmakers, woodworkers, and other artists and craftspeople were almost nonexistent. In Washington, the cultural revival that has accompanied the fishing-rights struggle has generated interest in traditional arts within Indian communities.[29] Again, long-distance communication and motor travel have helped this process by facilitating the Pan-Indianism of powwows and other intertribal gatherings, and Pan-Indianism, in turn, celebrates traditional expression by all Native American groups.

One folk art expression may give rise to another. The use of music and dance among Yakima Valley Mexican-Americans, for example, has stimulated a demand for costumes for the musicians and dancers. Many are ordered from the southwestern states or from Mexico, but some are made locally. Petra Jiménez of Toppenish, a fine needleworker, was once a dancer in the state of Jalisco, Mexico, and now makes elaborately embroidered dresses in the traditional style.[30]

Folk art may, as in the case of some Native American expressions, have economic benefits for whole communities, providing a source of income on remote and otherwise impoverished reservations. One outstanding example of the economic benefits of folk art in the modern world occurs among the Hmong refugees. These tribal people (also called Meo) left the highlands of Laos during the last years of the Indochina war and ended up in refugee camps in Thailand. Since the mid-1970s, many Hmong have settled in the United States. Most of those who came to Washington settled in Seattle or Spokane. For generations they have had a tradition of decorating their clothing with elaborate applique and embroidery. While they were in refugee camps, they developed a new form of folk art, the *paj ntaub* (usually transliterated as *pa ndau*) or "story cloth." This type of narrative tapestry typically depicts village life in the home country or the sequence of war, escape out of the hills, across the Mekong River to the camps in Thailand, and sometimes finally to the New World.[31] *Paj ntaub* has performed several important functions for the displaced Hmong people. It has been therapeutic, allowing its practitioners to confront national calamity in a way similar to the outpouring of literature spawned by the Holocaust. It has also become an important economic activity for destitute refugees, both in the camps and in American cities, where they have had no other marketable skills. Their economic success is a consequence of mainstream American fascination with this art. Hmong "story cloths" and appliqued panels are eminently salable in American cities, as a visit to Pike Place Market in Seattle will attest. Finally, the art has given recognition to Hmong-Americans, which is likely to foster respect and appreciation for people who might otherwise be ignored or rejected.

Despite the common assertion that folk art is "dying out," its demise is unlikely as long as it fulfills a function for its community. Certain kinds of folk art do die out; others are extremely tenacious. Still others, like Norwe-

Beadwork is a decorative art developed by Native Americans after Europeans introduced beads as trade goods. It is now done in Native American communities throughout the United States. In Washington it is more common among the Plateau peoples east of the Cascade Range. Cecilia Abrahamson (second from left in photo below), who lives near Ford, is the leading beadworker on the Spokane Reservation. She has made and decorated beautiful costumes worn by her daughters and granddaughters (with whom she is posing), who dance in powwows and other Native American gatherings.

(Photo courtesy of Cecilia Abrahamson.)

THEY LIVED IN PANANITKHOM ABOUT
SIX MOTHS THEN THEY PLEW TO AMERICA BY AN AIRLINER

The Hmong people of Southeast Asia have a long tradition of elaborate embroidery and applique. After the end of the Indochina War, most Hmong left their homeland in the Laotian mountains. While in refugee camps they developed a type of embroidered tapestry called paj ntaub, or "story cloth." Many Hmong refugees in the United States have been able to earn money making and selling their needlework. The Xiong family of Seattle sells at Pike Place Market. See Xiong (at right) sews while watching the market booth. A typical paj ntaub (above), by her mother, Yang Mee Xiong, narrates the story of war, displacement, and emigration.

48

gian *Rosemaling* or some of the Native American examples discussed above, have had cycles of near-extinction and subsequent revitalization. New forms of folk art occur, such as chainsaw carving among loggers or *paj ntaub* among the Hmong.

Social function is the sustaining force in folk artistic expression. Modern society is full of competing forms of expression, and people consciously choose some and reject others. As long as informally learned artistic expression is sustained by community aesthetic systems, there will be folk artists. The trend toward vicarious participation fostered by the mass media seems to be limited; people want to play music, carve figures, embroider. The rest of us value their work, sometimes for romantic reasons, sometimes because we share the aesthetic that their work expresses. ❖

NOTES

1   Washington's ethnic groups and the history of their settlement are discussed in detail in *Peoples of Washington*. Ed. Sid White and Sam Solberg. Pullman, WA: Washington State University Press, 1989. Articles about specific groups are indexed in *Bibliography of Washington State Folklore and Folklife: Selected and Partially Annotated*. Ed. Robert E. Walls. Seattle: University of Washington Press and Washington State Folklife Council, 1987.

2   The idea of a "high context" group is developed by Edward T. Hall in *Beyond Culture*. Garden City, NY: Doubleday, 1977. For its application to logging and other Northwest outdoor occupations, see J. Barre Toelken, *The Dynamics of Folklore*. Boston: Houghton-Mifflin Co., 1979, pp. 49-72.

3   Robert E. Walls' *Bibliography* indexes over 300 entries for "Logging" (pp. 266-67) and over fifty for "Logging Camps" (pp. 267-68). Vivid examples of the logger as a member of a high context group producing characteristic folklore (and other cultural expressions) can be found in the following works edited by Finley Hays and published by Loggers World Publications of Chehalis, WA: *Lies, Logs and Loggers*, 1961; *World of Loggers! By Many, Many Logging Authors*, 1966; and *Loggers World: The First Ten Years, 1964-1974*, 1987.

4   See Patricia Cooper and Norma Bradley Buford, *The Quilters: Women and Domestic Art*. Garden City, NY: Doubleday, 1977; Carrie Hall and Rose G. Kretsinger, *The Romance of the Patchwork Quilt in America in Three Parts*. 1935. Reprint. New York: Bonanza Books, 1969; and Patsy and Myron Orlofsky, *Quilts in America*. New York: McGraw-Hill Book Co., 1974. For a Washington perspective, see Diana McLachlan, *A Common Thread . . . Quilts in the Yakima Valley*. Yakima, WA: Yakima Valley Museum and Historical Association, 1985.

5   See *Instant Litter: Concert Posters From Seattle Punk Culture*. Ed. Art Chantry. Seattle: The Real Comet Press, 1985; and John Stamets, "Street Art," [Seattle] *Arts Line* 2:6 (October 1984), pp. 9-12.

6   Charles Camp, Review of *Folk Art of Idaho: "We Came to Where We Were Supposed to Be."* Ed. Steve Siporin. *Journal of American Folklore* 99:391 (January-March 1986), pp. 97-99. In addition to numerous works on the folk art of the southwestern states, three excellent catalogs of western state folk art are available. These are *Utah Folk Art*. Ed. Hal Cannon. Provo, UT: Brigham Young University Press, 1980; *Webfoots and Bunchgrassers: Folk Art of the Oregon Country*. Ed. Suzi Jones. Salem, OR: Oregon Arts Commission and University of Oregon Museum of Art, 1980 (also includes Washington examples, pp. 77, 118, 119); and *Folk Art of Idaho: "We Came to Where We Were Supposed to Be."* Ed. Steve Siporin. Boise, ID: Idaho Commission on the Arts, 1984 (Washington examples, pp. 95, 97).

7   See Jean Lipman and Alice Winchester, *The Flowering of American Folk Art (1776-1876)*. New York: Viking Press, 1974; and Jean Lipman, Elizabeth V. Warren, and Robert Bishop, *Young America: A Folk-Art History*. New York: Museum of American Folk Art/ Hudson Hills Press, 1987.

8   "What is Folk Art? A Symposium," *The Magazine Antiques* 57 (1950), pp. 355-62.

9   The best anthology of work by these newer scholars is *Folk Art and Art Worlds*. Ed. John Michael Vlach and Simon J. Bronner. Ann Arbor, MI: UMI Research Press, 1986. Also highly recommended are the following: Kenneth L. Ames, *Beyond Necessity: Art in the Folk Tradition*. Winterthur, DE: Henry Francis Du Pont Winterthur Museum, 1977; and *Perspectives on Folk Art*. Ed. Ian M.G. Quimby and Scott Swank. New York: W.W. Norton, 1980.

10   "Folk Art Meeting: Calm and Placid on the Surface . . ." [Library of Congress] *Folklife Center News* 7:1 (January-March 1984), pp. 4-5, 13. Good discussions of these issues can be found in Charlene Cerny, "Everyday Masterpieces," review of *Young America: A Folk Art History* by Jean Lipman *et al, New York Times Book Review*, December 10, 1987, pp. 15-16; Robert T. Teske, "What is American Folk Art?: An Opinion on the Controversy," *El Palacio: Magazine of the Museum of New Mexico* 88 (Winter 1983), pp. 34-38; and John Michael Vlach, "American Folk Art: Questions and Quandaries," *Winterthur Portfolio* 15 (1980), pp. 345-55.

11   I. Sheldon Posen and Daniel Franklin Ward, "Watts Towers and the Giglio Tradition," *Folklife Annual 1985*. Washington, D.C.: Library of Congress, American Folklife Center, 1985, pp. 143-56.

12   Warren E. Roberts, "Folk Crafts," in *Folklore and Folklife: An Introduction*, pp. 233-52. See also Glassie, "Folk Art," pp. 274-76; Charles Camp, *Traditional Craftsmanship in America: A Diagnostic Study*. Washington, D.C.: National Council on Traditional Arts, 1983; and Susan Sink, *Traditional Crafts and Craftsmanship in America: A Selected Bibliography*. Publications of the American Folklife Center, No. 11. Washington, D.C.: Library of Congress, American Folklife Center, 1983.

13   Washington's fairs and festivals are indexed in the *Washington Statewide Calendar of Events* distributed every March by the Washington State Department of Trade and Economic Development, AX 13, Tourism Development Division, Olympia, WA 98504. More complete calendars are *Bunney's Guide*, published every spring by Karen Bunney, P.O. Box 75565, Northgate Station, Seattle, WA 98125-0565, and *Washington Festival Directory and Resource Guide*, Ed. Judy Keyser, published annually by Puget Sound Festival Association, c/o Neighborhood Business Council, 500 Wall St. #206, Seattle, WA 98101.

14   See Henry Glassie, "Folk Art," in *Folklore and Folklife: An Introduction*. Ed. Richard M. Dorson. Chicago: University of Chicago Press, 1972, pp. 253-80 and the chapter, "Folk Crafts and Art," in Jan Harold Brunvand, *The Study of American Folklore: An Introduction*. Revised Edition. New York: W.W. Norton, 1978, pp. 319-34.

15   See Kimi Ota, *Sashiko Quilting*. Seattle: Privately published by Kimi Ota, 10300 61st Ave. S., Seattle, WA 98178.

16   Vance Horne, "Folk Art: Cultural Byproduct," and "Which Homemade Products are 'Folk Art'?" *The Olympian*, March 26, 1987, pp. 1C-4C.

17   See Vivian T. Williams, "Ag Art: Grange Agricultural Displays," *Seattle Folklore Society Journal* 3:3 (1972), pp. 2-7; and Gus Norwood, *Washington's Grangers Celebrate a Century*. Seattle: Washington State Grange, 1988, pp. 142-43. Available from Washington State Grange, 3104 Western Ave., Seattle, WA 98121-1073.

18   Fruit box labels are an interesting example of a shared folk aesthetic, although they are technically not folk art, but rather a form of commercial art associated with a particular occupational group. The labels are usually polychrome lithograph on paper. They originated in the citrus-growing areas of California during the 1920s. As fruit growing became important in the Northwest, apple growers and marketers developed their own decorative labels, many of which were made by German-born lithographers living in California. Some were also made in Seattle. Hundreds of different kinds were used by Washington growers and marketers from the 1920s through the 1950s, when they became extinct due to the adoption of the cardboard crate and the consolidation of marketing in cooperatives. They have, however, become an important part of the orchard region's shared aesthetic consciousness, and they are collected, traded, and sold like rare postage stamps. Many of the most avid collectors are themselves fruit ranchers. Most local museums and many restaurants in Central Washington display collections of labels, notably the Yakima Valley Museum and Historical Association in Yakima and the North Central Washington Museum in Wenatchee. See series

"Apple Box Art" by Mark Behler and Malcolm Keithley in [North Central Washington Museum, Wenatchee] *The Confluence*, 1984-86. See also Alan Taylor, "Yakima Valley Museum Catches Glimpses of Fruit Industry's Past," [Yakima] *The Goodfruit Grower*, March 15, 1978, pp. 2-4.

19   The meaning of woodcarving to older men is explored in Simon J. Bronner, *Chain Carvers: Old Men Crafting Meaning*. Lexington: University Press of Kentucky, 1985.

20   Kenneth C. Hansen, *The Maiden of Deception Pass: A Spirit in Cedar*. Anacortes: Samish Experience Productions, 1983, pp. 10-13.

21   Finley Hays, "John McKeekin: 'The Grays Harbor Pack Rat,' Aberdeen, Washington," *Loggers World* 22:11 (November 1986), pp. 34-42.

22   Elaine Frank Davison, "Some of the Customs of the Volga German Villages," [Omaha, NE] *Journal of the American Historical Society of Germans From Russia* 8:3 (1985), pp. 33-34.

23   Finley Hays, *Lies, Logs and Loggers, World of Loggers!,* and *Loggers World: The First Ten Years*. See also Steward H. Holbrook, *The Far Corner: A Personal View of the Pacific Northwest*. Reprint. Sausalito, CA: Comstock Editions, 1986; and *Holy Old Mackinaw*. New York: MacMillan, 1938; James Stevens, *Paul Bunyan*, 1925. Reprint. Sausalito, CA: Comstock Editions, 1986; and *Out of the Woods*. Seattle: University of Washington, Northwest Collection, 1957.

24   Harold Otto of Pateros, Oscar Herem of Deer Park, Bud Stewart of Smyrna, and Jim Hofer of Carson have distinguished themselves as cowboy poets. Leading Washington logger poets include Woodrow Gifford of Seaview, Linda Marcellus of Plain and Darcie Cunningham of Buckley (loggers' wives), Lon Minkler of Chehalis, Bill Iund of Winlock, N.B. Gardner, Sr., of Toutle, Jerry Brown of Tacoma, Ed Janhunen of Raymond, and Virgil Wallace of Amboy. Poems by Harold Otto and Jim Hofer appear in *Cowboy Poetry: A Gathering*. Ed. Hal Cannon. Layton, UT: Gibbs M. Smith/Peregrine-Smith Books, 1985, pp. 104-05, 148-51. Books of cowboy poetry by Washingtonians include Harold Otto, *Poems: Facts and fiction*. 1986. Privately published by Harold Otto, P.O. Box 343, Pateros, WA 98846; and Oscar Herem, *Ranch Reveries*. 1986. Privately published by Oscar Herem, P.O. Box 905, Deer Park, WA 99006. Books of logger poetry by Washingtonians include Woody Gifford, *Timber Bind: Logger Rhythms of the Great Northwest*. Chehalis, WA: Loggers World Publications, 1974; and Lon Minkler and Don Graham, *The Tall and the Uncut: Logging Poems and Cartoons*. Chehalis, WA: Loggers World Publications, 1976. Logger poems by Northwesterners appear regularly in the monthlies *Loggers World*, 4206 Jackson Hwy. S., Chehalis, WA 98532, and *American Timberman & Trucker*, P.O. Box 1006, Chehalis, WA 98532. Poems by Washington and Oregon fishermen appear in *Columbia River Gillnetter*, 322 Tenth St., Astoria, OR 97103.

25   For examples of ethnic ensembles in Washington, see this book's Appendix: Ethnic Resource Guide. Another good source is the monthly *Northwest Ethnic News*, published by the Ethnic Heritage Council of the Pacific Northwest, 3123 Eastlake E., Seattle, WA 98102; *Contact: Ethnic Heritage Directory*. 2 Vols. Seattle: Ethnic Heritage Council of the Pacific Northwest, 1981. Rev. ed. 1989; and Susan Auerbach, ed. & compiler, *The Directory of Ethnic Performers in Seattle*. Seattle: Ethnic Heritage Council of the Pacific Northwest, 1984. For Anglo-American music, see Woodrow R. Clevinger, "Southern Appalachian Highlanders in Western Washington," *Pacific Northwest Quarterly* 33:1 (1942): 3-45 and "The Appalachian Mountaineers in the Upper Cowlitz Basin," *Pacific Northwest Quarterly* 29:2 (1938): 115-134. Also see Vivian T. Williams, "The Washington Fiddlers Project," *The WashBoard* [Newsletter of the Washington State Folklife Council] 2:4/3:1 (Fall 1986/Winter 1987), pp. 1-5.

26   Wendy Bross Stuart, *Gambling Music of the Coast Salish Indians*. Mercury Series No. 3. Ottawa: National Museum of Man, 1972.

27   Bill Dietrich, "Washington's Indians" series. *The Seattle Times*, December 15-20, 1985.

28   "Petra Jiménez: Ella 'aprendió todo en México,'" [Seattle] *La Vóz*, April 1988, pp. 12-13.

29   Sally Peterson, "Translating Experience and the Reading of a Story Cloth," *Journal of American Folklore* 101:399 (January-March 1988), pp. 6-22; Virginia White, *Pa Ndau: The Needlework of the Hmong*. 1982. Privately published by Virginia White, 23 Sixth St., Cheney, WA 99004. ❖

In the first decade of this century, John Engfer of Orting immigrated to the Puyallup Valley from the German province of Pomerania, which is now a part of Poland, by way of Hawaii. As a boy in Washington, he learned from an older German immigrant to make traditional northeast German baskets, substituting vine maple for European ash on the frame, but using hazel wood for the strips, as was done in the old country. Some of the collectors who buy them request that he leave on the bark, as this makes them more evocatively "rustic." He has taught the craft to a neighbor, Frank Swalander, and these two gentlemen may be the last traditional European basketmakers in Washington.

"ISN'T THAT SOMETHING EVERYBODY KNOWS?": FOLK ART AND COMMUNITY

by Phyllis A. Harrison

Community" is a word folklorists find essential in describing folk traditions and the people who practice them. Artists typically say, "That's just the way we do it," "That's just how it's done," or, as cornhusk dollmaker Ada Whitmore of Soap Lake says, "Isn't that something everybody knows?" Behind every item of folk art is a sense of sharing and knowing, of belonging to a community that has fostered and passed on its folk traditions.

Folk traditions are created and maintained by individuals who pass their skills on to others informally, not through books or studios or galleries, but around kitchen tables, in living rooms, in fellowship halls and backyard workshops. These casual spaces house the communities where folklore exists as a meaningful part of daily life. Passed along from one person to another, folk tradition is rooted in and reflects the community's shared knowledge and history, common values, and concerns.

Until recently, folklorists explored rural villages and rustic settings for folk traditions, and regarded the items they found as survivals of a vanishing way of life. Now, we realize that folk traditions flourish in all kinds of communities. In fact, most of us are members of several of these communities, made up of individuals united by shared experience and knowledge. A community might be created by proximity—small towns, cities, or neighborhoods—or by age groups, such as teenagers or the elderly. The term also refers to gender groups (women's clubs, all male-hunting organizations), occupational groups (fishermen, wheat ranchers), religious affiliation, or ethnic background: in short, any situation that brings us into

Ada Whitmore of Soap Lake learned to make cornhusk dolls from her family when she was very young. Ordinary cornhusks are dyed, then sewn and glued together. Design seems to be limited only by imagination: "When you make one you've got ten more ideas in your head." Cornhusk dolls are found all over the world where corn is grown, especially in the American Midwest and in Eastern Europe. It is probably not a skill that has diffused from place to place. Instead, it may simply be a technique that is suggested by the physical qualities of the corn plant itself and is therefore subject to reinvention in many places.

regular contact with a group of people who share a particular bond. All these communities generate their own traditions: arts, crafts, customs, beliefs, stories, and expressions based on experiences and concerns of the group and passed along from person to person within it.

The close relationship between tradition and community often means that folk traditions are little known outside the community that fosters them. People often ask, "Where are these people?" or "How do you find folk artists?" Artists like those whose work you see in this volume are everywhere, and folklorists get to know them by going to the communities where they live and work. Much of a folklorist's work is field research, not accomplished in a library or at a desk, but in living rooms, backyards, kitchens, and workshops where we observe people at work and document their skills in situations where they are normally practiced, which we call "natural context." We visit churches, Grange halls, community, ethnic, and cultural centers, specialty shops, local gathering places like parks, corner grocery

54

The most traditional folk artists learn by direct interaction with older tradition-bearers. This is also the way their traditional skills are passed on to other people. Frank Swalander of Orting learned traditional basket-making skills from his neighbor John Engfer one severe winter when they were snowed in. Although Swalander has changed some of the characteristics of his baskets, and considers them an improvement over the way he learned to make them, he still considers them to be "usin' baskets, to haul potatoes, pack wood. You can't hurt 'em." Like Engfer's baskets, they are avidly sought by collectors, although they were once purely utilitarian.

stores, and coffee shops, senior centers, nursing homes, student clubs, and local events—any place where people with common interests get together to do business and socialize.

"Context" means that folklorists are interested not only in the artifact itself, but in what that artifact means to the artist and to the community: how the item—the quilt, the proverb, the fiddle, the tune—is created and used. Where and from whom did the artist learn the skills? Where and how does the artist obtain raw materials? Who uses the items? Are they sold, traded, given as gifts? How do potential users learn about them? Does the artist have students or apprentices? Who passes judgment on the quality of the item, and by what criteria?

One example of the significance of context is found in the basket-weaving of two men in the Puyallup Valley. John Engfer came from

Thorleif (Tom) Hageland's clocks are elaborately carved and scrollwork-sawn. Some have wooden works. Hageland comes from several generations of Norwegian woodcarvers and remembers his father as a master "jackknife carver." In addition to clocks, he also carves gunstocks, human figures, and animals. He moved to Bremerton from Montana twenty-five years ago.

56

Pomerania in Eastern Germany (now Western Poland) and settled in the Valley in the early 1900s. He and his fellow immigrants brought basket-making skills to their hop farms in the Valley. Frank Swalander was born in the Valley and has lived near Orting all his life. Forty years ago during a winter snowstorm, Engfer taught Swalander how to make the baskets they used on their farms. Swalander has made a few changes in the design, but he still follows the traditional process. Both men collect wild hazel and vine maple from nearby woods to use for baskets, many of which are given or sold to family, friends, and neighbors. Their baskets were featured at The Governor's Invitational Art Exhibitions in 1987 and 1988, and in an article in *Country Living Magazine.* This publicity broadened their market considerably, but their primary form of advertising is still word of mouth, periodic displays on Swalander's front porch, and an occasional entry in the Western Washington State Fair in Puyallup.

Proximity brought these two men together, and most of their work remains in Pierce and southern King counties. Orting is proud of its basketmakers, and the two men are justifiably proud of their work. Their baskets are more than attractive homemade artifacts: they represent the history and culture of a self-sufficient rural community that used—and still uses—local materials and skills to meet local needs. They represent a practical view of the world. Swalander describes his baskets as "Usin'

For the past two decades, about twenty women of the Mission Circle Quilt Group of the Glad Tidings Assembly of God in Darrington have met every other Thursday to piece and sew quilts. Small groups of six or less gather around quilt frames to sew or cut fabric. Some of the quilts are given to needy families in the area, but most are sent away to Assembly of God missionaries. Many of the women quilted before joining the group, but Christian fellowship is the group's stated goal. "That's what it's all about—the fellowship when we quilt." Margie Black, Christine Sonntag, and Lucille Morgan are quilting here.

baskets. You can haul potatoes or pack wood in them . . . you can't hurt them." They also represent a changing environment and economy in which raw materials are more difficult to come by and in which sturdy baskets that once hauled potatoes now grace the shelves of folk art collections. Finally, they represent the shared experiences and knowledge of two men in rural Pierce County.

Religious groups create another kind of community, and provide an appropriate context for traditional arts. The Mission Circle Quilt Group of Darrington has met weekly at the Glad Tidings Assembly of God since the church was established twenty years ago. Some of the women were accomplished quilters before joining the group, while others have learned to quilt since they joined. The quilts go to needy families in the area and to missionaries; the quilting provides financial assistance to the church and fellowship for the quilters.

Families are another kind of community, and often generate their own traditions. Special holiday meals, customs and celebrations, family stories, and anecdotes passed from person to person strengthen family ties and enliven the family tree. The sustained, intimate, and informal circumstances of family life can provide an ideal setting for the transmission of folklore. Kathy Peterson of Arlington learned to crochet rugs by watching her grandmother; Hazel Holm of Darrington learned to tat by watching her mother and taking instruction from a cousin; Thorleif (Tom) Hageland of Bremerton learned woodcarving from his father. Family ties often provide the first link in the human chain of folk tradition.

Ethnicity is also a source of community, one that belies images of melting pots and average Americans. Many Washingtonians maintain traditions from their homelands. Stepping into Tacoma's Cambodian Buddhist Temple, for example, is like stepping into another world. From the outside, one sees a modest single-story frame house. Inside, however, the visitor sees shoes shed by the door, smells Cambodian foods being prepared in the kitchen, and walks through a hallway decorated with prints representing the complex blend of Buddhism, Hinduism, and animism observed by this sect. In the sanctuary, where services are held and the monks eat their ritual meals, nearly every bit of space on the walls, the ceiling, and the altar is filled with religious pictures and images, with handmade artifacts like the *tuong proleang* (spirit flags or prayer flags), with candles, flowers, and beads —all part of religious services and ceremonies, and all as familiar to the Cambodian community as the cross to Christians or the menorah to Jews. The temple is a place of worship, but also a place of familiar sights, sounds, and traditions for those who worship there. It provides spiritual sustenance and a bit of precious familiarity for a group of people newly transplanted to a very different world.

The term "ethnic" does not always mean "immigrant." Native Americans form a multitude of distinct communities whose traditions have

The altar and the tuong proleang *(spirit flags or prayer flags) in the Cambodian Buddhist Temple of Tacoma provide an atmosphere of familiarity as well as spiritual inspiration for Cambodian refugees in that city.* Tuong proleang *are pieced and embroidered by older women of the congregation. They are decorated according to the tastes of their makers and given to the Temple for display.*

helped unify members in the midst of tremendous cultural incursions and upheavals. For example, Edith Bedal, a Sauk Indian who lives in Darrington, learned basketmaking from her mother at a time when all young Sauk girls learned the craft. They collected their materials—cedar bark, cedar root, bear grass, cherry bark, and fern root—from local streams and forests. The baskets were used for daily cooking, transporting, and storage, and were sometimes taken as far as Seattle for sale or trade. Bedal still gathers her own materials, though logging and private property have made access more difficult and some of her raw materials now come from the Forest Service and from lumber mills. Many of her baskets are owned and used by family, friends, and other Sauk. Aware that these skills might otherwise disappear, Bedal teaches classes in basketmaking at the Sauk-Suiattle Tribal Center. "It is a wonderful tradition," she observes, "but if they don't learn it, it will die out completely." The tradition involves more than the baskets. It embodies an intimate knowledge of and relationship to the land and its resources. It articulates the self-sufficiency of a Native community that produced goods from available resources and traded those goods for other necessities, including cash. It is also the expression of generations of Sauk women who, in the course of daily life, passed their skills on to younger generations.

Demographic, technological, and environmental changes sometimes

Sauk Indian basketmaker Edith Bedal of Darrington learned to make traditional Sauk baskets from her mother, Susie Bedal, during early childhood. As a young girl, her job was to do the finishing work on her mother's baskets. Today, her daughters also make baskets, having learned from their mother. Among the Sauk people, basketmaking skills are traditionally transmitted from mother to daughter. The baskets are typically made of split cedar root, and decorated with bear grass and sometimes cherry bark; some are made so tightly that they can be used for cooking. Bedal has been a leader in preservation of Sauk traditions, teaching basketmaking at the Tribal Center, translating minutes of tribal meetings, and collecting oral histories. Her fine craftsmanship and artistic sense, as well as her work to preserve Sauk culture, earned her a Governor's Award of Commendation in 1988.

Cy Williams of the Tulalip Tribe has produced many monumental wood sculptures on public display in Western Washington. Some are inspired by Tulalip tradition, others by the traditions of the northern Indian nations of the British Columbia and southeast Alaska coasts, and still others are entirely personal. Many contemporary Native American wood-sculptors rough out their work with a chainsaw and finish with hand tools.

threaten the stability of folk groups, and ethnic communities face additional pressure from a dominant culture not always sympathetic to diversity. These communities often make use of a variety of cultural resources. The Tulalips of Marysville, for example, have turned to teachers and artists within their community and to the legacy of artifacts from previous generations to revitalize the practice of their traditional arts. They have also drawn upon the recollections of elders, on museum collections, books on Northwest Indian art, and the resources of their tribes, shared through powwows and the Tulalip Treaty Festival, which bring together Native Americans from throughout the Northwest.

Clyde Williams, Sr. grew up with Tulalip carvers and carving, though he does not recall one specific teacher. When he began carving on his own, he drew upon traditional knowledge, personal creativity, books, and museum pieces for inspiration. Like many Native American carvers, he has sold his work outside the community in response to art market demands for Northwest Indian work. Still, much of his carving remains in the hands of family and tribal members, and he was asked by the tribe to carve one of the poles which now stands in front of the Tribal Center.

Neither Cy Williams nor Chuck Campbell grew up on the Tulalip Reservation, but both live and work there now, carving totem poles along the highway near Lynch's Trading Post. Using chainsaws for much of the work and hand carving for finishing details, they create traditional Tulalip designs as well as less traditional designs. Cy Williams learned to carve from his grandfather, an uncle, and several cousins, using an adze, drawknives, and chisels. The chainsaw, which he began using in the early 1970s, allows him to work with greater speed and to use wood he could not work with hand tools. Chuck Campbell has learned primarily from Williams. The market for their work includes Tulalips, other Native Americans (Williams

Norwegian immigrants Solveig and Emile Indrebo of Tacoma distinguished themselves as ethnic artists. Solveig Indrebo learned to spin in Norway as a girl, and still demonstrates at ethnic fairs and craft shows. Emile Indrebo made his first violin in Norway as a boy of twelve, and continued making them occasionally during the years he worked as a logger in Brooklyn, Washington. During the years between his retirement in 1972 and his death in 1988, he made forty-two Hardingfele or "Hardanger fiddles." These elaborate violins are characteristic of the Hardanger district in Western Norway. Their elaborate inlays and carvings are highly visible, but the distinguishing technical feature of the Hardingfele is the presence of four extra strings that pass through tubes in the neck and resonate sympathetically when the four regular strings are played, giving the instrument remarkable acoustic amplification.

carved and painted one of the totem poles at the Puyallup Tribal Center in Tacoma), non-Indian residents of the area, and summer tourists.

Shannon Pablo, also of the Tulalips, describes herself as a self-taught beadworker, though much of her skill comes from growing up with the work of other Tulalip beadworkers. Most of the baby-boards, earrings, and moccasins she creates remain on the reservation, although she occasionally sells her work elsewhere. Raymond Fryberg, Sr. is a drummaker. Inspired by longstanding family involvement in Native American religious activities, he acquired drummaking skills on his own and with the help of other Native Americans at powwows in different parts of the West. He uses his drums at powwows and at Tulalip events and in such ceremonies as the June "Welcoming of the First Salmon," revived in 1978 by Tulalip Stan Jones, Sr. By 1988, this ceremony involved not only the Tulalip community but also visitors from other tribes and from the non-Indian community, including a reporter from *National Geographic* magazine.

Washington's Norwegian citizens also exemplify the vitality of ethnic traditions in the state. Solveig Indrebo and her late husband, Emile, of Tacoma, were born in Norway and came to this country during the 1920s. Emile Indrebo built *Hardingfele* or "Hardanger fiddles"—violins originating in the Hardanger district of Western Norway. The instruments are distinguished by elaborate decoration and eight strings—four "stopped" strings for playing and four resonating understrings to enhance the sound. Indrebo built his first fiddle at age twelve in Norway with the help of a schoolteacher. Here in Washington, after retiring from logging, he took up fiddlemaking again, and corresponded with a cousin in Norway who also made fiddles. Most of his instruments belong to members of the local Scandinavian community. Solveig Indrebo also brought Norwegian skills to Washington. As a young girl in Norway, she learned to spin—"We all had to learn," she recalls—and she still spins yarn, which she knits and crochets into items for family and friends. She obtains most of her wool from relatives in Montesano who raise sheep, and though Douglas fir needles embedded in the wool make it hard to clean, she cleans and cards it for spinning. In addition to sharing their creations with the local Scandinavian population, the Indrebos gave regular demonstrations at Scandinavian festivals and gatherings in the area.

Elene Emerson, a second-generation Norwegian-American, learned *Hardangersøm*—a style of stitching involving counted pulled threads— through Tacoma's Daughters of Norway Lodge. Her teacher was a first-generation immigrant from Hardanger, Norway. Emerson has made doilies, table runners, and wall pieces for herself, family, and friends, and collars, cuffs, and apron-and-bodice trim for her own daily use and for the costumes she wears to lodge events. She has several students, also members of the lodge, who meet weekly in her home to practice the intricate *Hardangersøm* work.

Al and Nora Anderson's tine *(Norwegian oval boxes) are part of a family craft tradition brought by the Anderson family to the United States from Norway. Al Anderson learned from his Norwegian-born father, who moved to Tacoma from Wisconsin. He and his wife now make them at their home in Wauna.* Tine *were used in Norway as lunch boxes for farmers and herders. Like most traditional baskets, they have been transmuted from utility to art, and today they are collected and displayed by heritage-conscious Norwegian-Americans. Al Anderson is also a skilled cabinetmaker and basketmaker.*

Al and Nora Anderson of Wauna, also second-generation Norwegians, practice another traditional Norwegian craft. Al Anderson's father, Nikolas, came from Norway, where he learned to make *tine* or *loupe* (covered oval baskets of bent wood) and *korge* (round wooden baskets). He brought his skills to the United States, arriving in Tacoma in 1897, where he continued to make *tine* and *korge* for his family, friends, and associates. Many of his pieces are still used by Norwegians in the Tacoma area. Al Anderson learned to make *tine* as a small boy by helping his father. His years of millwork left little time for his own woodworking, but after retiring, he again began to make *tine*. Although he has made few changes in the design, he can still recognize his father's boxes when he sees them. Nora Anderson works with her husband, and many of their *tine* go to Pierce County *rosemalere* or to Norwegian friends, though some are sold in local galleries. Al Anderson has taught one of his sons and a neighbor boy to make the oval boxes.

The community of these artists is clearly quite different from the community of Nikolas Anderson or even the community that the Indrebos found when they arrived. Turn-of-the-century Tacoma was the home of many first-generation Norwegians. They often spoke Norwegian as their primary language, and associated primarily with other Norwegians. The Andersons both spoke Norwegian as children, and Nora Anderson remembers that Sunday school and church services in Cromwell were always held in Norwegian. Now that English has supplanted Norwegian and the Norwegian community has dispersed, lodges like the Sons of Norway and the Daughters of Norway, festivals celebrating Norwegian and Scandinavian culture, and the work of artisans like the Andersons, the Indrebos, and Elene Emerson keep the Norwegian community alive and give meaning and value to the ethnic traditions of their members.

The fact of change in ethnic communities has raised questions for the folklorist. How should traditions be regarded when the person-to-person, multiple-generation process is not clear-cut? In order to deal with the change in traditional patterns, we ask many of the same questions discussed earlier to identify community involvement with the artist. Are the artists familiar with predecessors and their work, or do they learn from books written by scholars outside the community? Does the item (or custom or tale or song) have a place in the community, or is it used or sold only to outsiders? Do the artists and the community set standards, or is the work evaluated only by outsiders? No community exists in isolation, and the task of identifying folk tradition often involves delineating community and outside involvement and deciding where, on a spectrum ranging from "folk" to "non-folk," a particular tradition belongs. The Tulalips, for example, form a discrete social, geographic, and political entity. Despite outside visitors and markets, despite the self-taught designations of several of their artists, the community base of Tulalip traditions argue for their placement on the "folk" end of the spectrum.

The concept of community is crucial to the study of folk traditions. For the artist, community is a fact of life. Folklorists analyze and label in order to better understand how folk traditions work in the lives of the people who maintain them. The categories we use often overlap, and like all students of human behavior, we often find gray areas. Structures and systems that mesh neatly in the lecture hall do not always fit precisely when one takes them into the field—to the homes and workshops where people practice folk traditions as part of the business of living. Many ethnic traditions are also family traditions. Native American traditions often have family, ethnic, and geographic bases. Changes in technology affect us all, and most artisans will use the best materials and tools available, whether they are the chisels and mallets of the turn-of-the-century stonecarver, or the power-driven points of his contemporary counterpart. Innumerable influences affect folk traditions and probably always have, but one constant element in traditional life is the person-to-person, community-based process through which folk artists have learned their skills, created their works, and shared them with others. ❖

Dawn Grytness operates the Mahaffey Camp Store on the Kalama River in Cowlitz County. In between waiting on customers, she ties the steelhead flies that have earned her a regional reputation. The walls of the store are decorated with Polaroids of successful catches.

MAKING SOMETHING OUT OF "NOTHING"

by Janet C. Gilmore

*I*t is a slow afternoon at Mahaffey Camp Store, up the Kalama River. Proprietor Dawn Grytness is perched at her fly-tying station, finishing up a "Deer-Hair Caddis." A couple of young sports fishermen come in, returning from a day on the river. Grytness jumps up to greet them, tend the cash register, monitor the gas pump, and supervise their progress as they roam the store for snacks, all the while bantering with them about the success of their fishing. An elderly neighbor woman drops by to see if the newspaper has come yet. Two young girls arrive with a small handful of coins and ask Grytness what sweet the money will buy. A few late-starting fishing regulars breeze in to buy a six-pack. For a time, the store buzzes with locals picking out supplies, asking questions, making comments about events of local significance. Friends appear on the scene and linger, squeezing in conversation between Grytness' exchanges with customers. When all is quiet again, Grytness finishes the fly and starts another, this time a "Crystal Flame." A greenhorn camper drops in, despairing about a forgotten can opener and cooking gear. Grytness dispenses culinary advice while locating spare utensils to loan him. More fishermen check in, survey the fishing tackle, help themselves to bait, and ask how the fishing has been going. The neighbor returns to ask about the paper, and soon her husband joins her. The children follow with another cache of pennies. In two hours, Grytness has completed two flies.

Grytness attracts customers by providing basic supplies and services. Central to the livelihood of her store, located in a popular year-round southwestern Washington sports fishing area, is the availability of a good range of locally proven fishing tackle and supplies. But in order to compete successfully with other well-stocked suppliers in the area, Grytness has had to develop a distinctive act that will attract a clientele. She takes a personal interest in her customers, greeting them as they enter, inquiring after them as they rummage about the store, offering advice, and encouraging them to return with reports of the outcome of a campfire recipe, a fishing trip, or a job search. She papers the store's walls with photographs of fishermen with their catches, of loggers, truck drivers, and other regulars. She makes their business her business.

By attracting repeat customers who share concerns, successes, and failures with her, she enhances her ability to serve. She learns, in particular, where fish are biting and what tackle is working, which flies are the most popular, and which fishermen are the luckiest. By keeping up with current fishing conditions and trends, she can offer up-to-date news and advice based on the experiences of many. The fact that she can tie flies secures her position as a sports fishing authority.

Grytness grew up in Idaho, where her father "raised me to fish." Later she and her husband spent their leisure time fishing streams, rivers, and lakes in Idaho, Oregon, and Washington. After she and her husband retired, moved to the Kalama River, and bought the store, Grytness learned to tie flies from her brother, who in turn had learned from their father. She says that her first flies were "pretty crude, but they caught fish." She expanded and refined her skills with the help of her brother's son and an expert local fly-tier, "Blackie" Tidd, who worked upriver at Pritchard's Store. His mentor was the late Al Pritchard, a local fly-fisherman. Soon Grytness was helping Blackie fill orders for flies whenever the fishing was so hot that customers were waiting in line for them. She eventually began producing flies for her own store, and has passed her skills on to her daughter.

Grytness would acknowledge that she has become proficient at tying flies, but she is modest about her ability, reserving the distinction of "artist" for Blackie, who she says is "second to none at fly-tying." She points out that not only is he a master of technique, but he is an innovator. His flies have received wide acclaim, and he uses fly-tying materials to create whimsical creatures, usually representing local wildlife. In contrast, Grytness sees herself as merely capable of reproducing the work of others. But she is clearly an artist, too. She has not yet created original patterns herself, but she can quickly and expertly reproduce any fly that a customer brings in. Furthermore, she no longer ties flies that will simply catch fish, but executes with finesse ones that will effectively "catch the eye of the fisherman."[1]

Because of her lifelong experience as a fly-fisher and her interest in fly-tying, Grytness can back up her flies with appropriate pedigrees. She knows their names, patterns, and stories of their origins, development, and popularity—whether the design is original, like the "Crystal Flame," or whether it "goes way back," like the "Kalama Special." She knows which flies work best for different fish in different seasons and water conditions, and more importantly, which ones work best for different fishermen. She says that newcomers to the area or the sport like to buy colorful flies with local names like the "Kalama Dyn-O-Mite," while "purists" prefer to style their own. Grytness is also familiar with the work of peer artists. She knows the people in the area who tie flies. She can discuss their skills, their styles,

Theodore (Tete) Lugnet of Ilwaco has been fishing commercially since early childhood. He describes himself as a man who has always "fooled around with knots," learning some of them from a friend, a former merchant seaman, with whom he fished. He always used slack times to sharpen his ropework skills, and in recent years has come to specialize in making ropework picture frames, an idea he first learned about from the encyclopedic Ashley Book of Knots. *As a fisherman who made and repaired his own nets, his artistic expression is a direct result of his occupational skills.*

and the philosophies behind their techniques. And she can also place her work in the historical line of local fly-tiers and within the contemporary circle of enthusiasts in the Northwest.

In many ways, Grytness is a model folk artist. She acquired her fly-tying skills from peers and elders, refined them through practice and personal experience, and adapted them to her local context. She also used the skills to carve a niche for herself and her store. Her popularity, and her daughter's adoption of the skill, are measures of her achievement in meeting the demands of her public and gaining acceptance among fellow fly-tiers.

Her example illustrates how folk art serves jointly personal and social functions. Fly-tying fascinates her, and through it she participates actively in her community and contributes to its social and economic vitality. Through her art, she does something for herself and simultaneously for others.

Grytness cites simple reasons for doing what she does— operating the store because she and her husband "were not busy enough," learning to tie flies because her children encouraged her to do so. These rationales are classic: they define the primary motivations of folk artists in Washington State and throughout the country. Most folk artists are people who "can't just sit and do nothing," as quilter Hazel Thompson Montague of Bellingham says. Faced with a spare moment at work or at home, or after retirement, they must do something, some *thing*, with their hands.[2] Frequently, they turn to skills practiced at home or on the job over a lifetime, applying them to new ends, elevating them from the routine, making art out of the ordinary.

Betty Robertson Russell of Bellingham, for example, was a professional seamstress, as were her mother and grandmother before her. After she retired, she took up fancy quiltmaking, delighting in experimenting with colors and designs in ways that tailoring and dressmaking had not offered. Similarly, Theodore (Tete) Lugnet, who calls himself a "double-decked squarehead" because of his Finnish and Swedish heritage, turned rope-tying skills into an art. He had learned to tie basic knots "naturally," in woods- and water-related jobs in the Ilwaco area. During slow times on his commercial fishing boat, he began practicing knots with his partner, a sometime merchant seaman who had picked up knot lore on seagoing expeditions. After Lugnet's boat "blew up" and he decided to retire, he began decorating picture frames with intricate combinations of common knots. On the one hand, he found it interesting to apply his rope-tying skills to knots he would not normally produce for work; on the other hand, he found it intriguing to juxtapose basic knots in uncommon arrangements for aesthetic effect.

A sense of experimentation and play is essential in the creation of fanciful things, leavening the burden of time, tasks, and the ordinary. As Blanche Anderson Manchester of Bellingham says of her quilting, "It's fun

A long career as a commercial fisherman inspired Andrew J. Evich of Bellingham to build models of commercial fishing boats, such as purse seiners, draggers, and gillnetters. The slack season from December through March was, before his retirement, the period during which he built models. To some extent, model-building was a way for him to experiment with the rigging and arrangement of fishing gear aboard the real boats on which he worked. One of his purse seiners was an expression of the ideal boat he would have liked to own. The models he made for himself were built "just like a real boat, from the keel up." In recent years, he has started making smaller, carved models for friends. Like many Washington commercial fishermen, Evich is the son of Croatian immigrants.

to see what's going to come out." An element of challenge is also important. One of Manchester's projects, for example, involved piecing a quilt top of hundreds of two-inch cloth hexagons, each of which featured a different print in brown colors. It was stimulating to accumulate the necessary scraps and to imagine the finished overall pattern.

Netherlands-born Ida Kooy Hempel of Lynden enjoys figuring out how to make things from scraps and materials she has on hand. "I like to make something out of nothing," she says. For a time, she turned out volumes of knitted slippers in a pattern she learned as a child, using yarn made of retired nylon stockings cut into rounds and looped together. She has crocheted rugs out of strips cut from plastic bags, and she braids rugs with good cloth in worn wool clothing, sewing the braids together with the "yarn" made from nylon stockings.

"You see a pattern, it looks nice, you try it," says Dena Hobbelink Huisman Johnston, a knitter of fine lace trims and doilies, also of Lynden, also born in the Netherlands. Like Hempel, who is "always looking for something to do," she likes to test her needlework skill by seeing if she can execute a new design or technique that she has dreamed up or watched another artist perform.

This kind of challenge not only keeps handwork interesting, but it also maintains and hones skills, training the mind as well as the hands. "It makes you think," says Andrew Evich of Bellingham about his craft. During seasonal lulls, the Croatian-American commercial fisherman built a couple of scale models, fully fitted out, of local types of commercial fishing vessels. The task helped him think through the parts of the fishing boat so that he could comprehend their interrelationships and the procedures necessary for maintaining and repairing his own boat.

Instead of modeling the purse seiner he owned at the time, Evich first built a beam trawler, and later a model of the kind of purse seiner he would have liked to operate. For him, model-building served partly to fulfill dreams. For many artists, the creation of artifacts not only stimulates the mind, but calms it, as well. Needleworkers, especially, report that handwork helps them relax, or contemplate, or "keep on even keel," by taking their minds off their troubles. Betty Russell calls her work "a kind of therapy." The familiar rhythm of the work, the progression through a finite and predetermined series of steps, the acts of completion, bestow a sense of order and control that can help sublimate frustration with the realities of everyday life.[4]

One of the finest and most productive quilters in Bellingham is surrounded by a house continually being remodeled, a garden laden with produce, a porch and kitchen overwhelmed with canning supplies, a dining-room table stacked with projects and paperwork for community service, and a living room filled with quilts in all stages of completion draped over mazes of quiltmaking equipment and materials. Handwork

As a boy in Hamm, Germany, a town on the Netherlands border, Otto Franz Stieber learned detailed woodworking on a small scale. After moving to Whatcom County near Lynden, he worked in many trades, including coal mining, logging, and building construction. During the Bicentennial, he was asked to build model wagons to commemorate a celebrative wagon train from Blaine to Washington, D.C. Since then, he has used the skills he learned during his childhood to make hundreds of model wagons, as well as models of coal mines, logging operations, and pioneer villages.

allows artists, especially women who may have lost themselves in years of child-rearing and housework, a time to themselves, a chance to do something just for themselves. Betty Russell confirms her daughter Julie's opinion that quiltmaking gives her a sense of identity and accomplishment, "something that is hers."

Rarely does the artist work entirely for herself, however. She needs additional motivation: the encouragement of family or friends, or a special family or community event. Mothers, grandmothers, and great-aunts are often moved to resurrect skills learned much earlier in life in honor of births, graduations, and marriages. The birth of a daughter to her favorite niece prompted rag-rug-weaver Enola Paddock Gillaspie of Longview to create a quilt of embroidered blocks for the child.[5] Preparations for the West-to-East Covered Wagon Train originating at Blaine during the Bicentennial inspired Otto Stieber to build a few scale models of the wagons. Encouraged by the positive community response, he began building models to compete in local parades and fairs, and to display in Lynden Pioneer Museum festivities. He replicated wagons he had seen as a boy in northwestern Germany, and in his work in mining in Eastern Washington and in farming, land-clearing, sawmilling, road-paving, and bricklaying in Whatcom

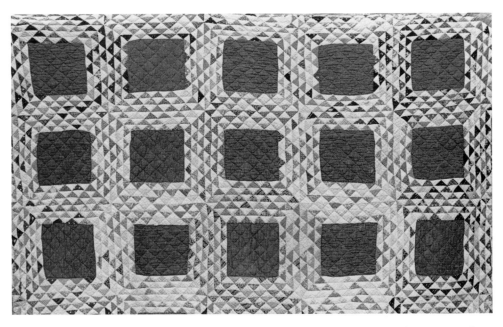

Dorothy Wooldridge Person of Battle Ground is descended from at least four generations of fine needleworkers and lacemakers. The "ocean waves" quilt was made by her great-grandmother, Elvira Williams Gregory, as was the Battenburg lace collar (upper right) and the crocheted antimacassar (lower right). The Battenburg lace doily is by Person herself. She keeps a substantial collection of ancestral needlework and lace as a kind of artifactual family history. She quilts, crochets, and makes both Battenburg and bobbin lace.

County. Stieber and his wife Sylvia have proudly decorated an entire wall of their living room with the trophies, ribbons, certificates of honor and achievement, and photographs that he has garnered for his work.

While public presentation of their work provides Stieber and others like him with recognition of their artistic skills, it also offers them a chance to exchange the solitude of the workshop for stimulating interaction with an admiring public and fellow handworkers. Sociability likewise underlies the work of artists who use their skills to participate in charitable community organizations. The women of the Martha Circle of the United Congregational Church in Naselle weave rag rugs all year to raise money for the church at the annual Christmas Bazaar and Naselle's biennial Finnish-American Folk Festival. From clothing donated for rugmaking, the weavers also sew coverlets for Baloney Joe's, a relief organization for the homeless in Portland. Yet the coffee break—when needleworking ceases and no cash is raised—is no less an important part of the weekly work day; it is an opportunity to share homemade breads and pastries, recipes, and good conversation. Like many women who gather regularly to produce coverlets for the Red Cross, or men who reassemble "Toys for Tots," their work has a dual purpose: it fulfills a need to help others and offers a chance to be part of a community.

The choice of what skill to practice has social as well as artistic implications. Indeed, folk artists select their company, the special people associated with their art, as carefully as they would a grain of wood or a swatch of cloth. By establishing their affiliations, by designating mentors and peers, they define themselves.

Dorothy Wooldridge Person of Battle Ground uses quilting to define her family line and her place within it. By producing her own quilts she maintains a family skill inherited from her mother, grandmother, and great-grandmother, and she participates in a family activity even though not all of the participants are physically present. By completing quilts that her mother began and embroidering them with her name alongside her mother's as co-creators, she recalls her mother's presence and influence, and celebrates their relationship. By teaching her skills to her daughter and grand-daughter, she perpetuates the art and the female family line. By preserving, repairing, and documenting the quilts made by the women in her family, she creates a historical record of the dynasty in artifacts, and registers her position in the line. In preparing and presenting a recent exhibit of her family's six generations of quilts, which included a photograph and short biography of each quilter, she made a powerful public statement about the longevity of her family in the area, its status as an original pioneer family, its link with the region's mythic past, and, accordingly, its importance in shaping the character of the region.[6]

The late Fred Marquand discovered his community on the waterfront in Bellingham during the last days of sail-powered shipping. As a boy,

Marquand found the shipyards and canneries and the seamen tattooing themselves more inspiring than art classes in high school. He learned to tattoo by watching the old salts decorate themselves with blue pigs, roosters, and dragons, using sharpened bamboo sticks. When they weren't looking, he would test their tools on himself. Marquand never did go to sea, but he became absorbed in tattooing. He eventually set up his own shop, inked full-scale facsimiles of the designs in his repertoire to display to customers, and perfected the tattooing machine. He tattooed hundreds of customers, and received tattoos all over his body from peer artists throughout the Northwest. His fading tattoos recorded his connections with other great tattooers and the times and places he knew them. They reminded him of the days of sail, the vibrant waterfront, and the old sailors who were gone. Through the record of his tattoos, he relived the extraordinary times in his life and entered the company of the people who fascinated him.[7]

Marquand's tattoos and Person's quilts are examples of using basic traditional hand skills to "make something out of nothing," to make art by elevating the ordinary to the extraordinary. But even more importantly, that "something," their folk art, also renders the extraordinary near and tangible. Beyond celebrating the power and beauty of an everyday pattern or stitch, folk art taps wells of fond memories and proud associations that come rarely in a lifetime. Through folk art, the artist fuses the ordinary and the extraordinary to create a living past—a personal mythology—to convey to contemporaries and generations yet to come.[8] ❖

NOTES

1   Steve Siporin makes a nice statement of this principle in his introduction to *Folk Art of Idaho: "We Came to Where We Were Supposed to Be."* Ed. Steve Siporin. Boise, ID: Idaho Commission on the Arts, 1984, p. 4. See also Barre Toelken's discussion of the (im)practicality of Nez Perce deerskin saddles in his "In the Stream of Life: An Essay on Oregon Folk Art," in *Webfoots and Bunchgrassers: Folk Art of the Oregon Country.* Ed. Suzi Jones. Salem, OR: Oregon Arts Commission and the University of Oregon Museum of Art, 1980, pp. 27-28.

2   Jane C. Beck illustrates this point in her essay, "Always in Season: Folk Art and Traditional Culture in Vermont," in *Always in Season: Folk Art and Traditional Culture in Vermont.* Ed. Jane C. Beck. Montpelier, VT: Vermont Council of the Arts, 1982, p. 25. See also James P. Leary and Janet C. Gilmore, "Cultural Forms, Personal Visions," in *From Hardanger to Harleys: A Survey of Wisconsin Folk Art.* Ed. Robert Teske. Sheboygan, WI: John Michael Kohler Arts Center, 1987, pp. 16-17.

3   See also Gary Stanton, "Whimsey and Recreation," in *Folk Art of Idaho,* p. 63.

4   See similar statements in Toelken, "In the Stream of Life," p. 31, and in Gary Stanton, "Beauty in the Home," in *Folk Art of Idaho,* p. 98.

5   See also Harry Gammerdinger, "Ceremony and Celebration," in *Folk Art of Idaho,* p. 88.

6   See Toelken, "In the Stream of Life," p. 31.

7   For some lovely embellishments of this point, see Beck, "Always in Season," pp. 25-28; Suzi Jones, "Pioneers," in *Webfoots and Bunchgrassers,* p. 69; and Gary Stanton, "Beauty in the Home," p. 10.

8   See also Leary and Gilmore, "Cultural Forms, Personal Visions," p. 22.

Walter (Buzz) Culbert of Pasco was one of the leading welders in the Hanford-Tri-Cities nuclear complex. He began his welding career in Seattle's shipyards, and first tried his hand at artistic metal sculpture around 1930. He later refined his skills to the exacting specifications of the nuclear industry, and eventually began making realistic representations of such natural objects as leaves, branches, and flowers. He taught welding for decades and in his later years taught other welders how to create artistic compositions. The high degree of welding skill demanded by the nuclear industry lends itself to the minuteness of fine artistic welding.

HONORING WORK: OCCUPATIONAL FOLK ART IN WASHINGTON

by Harry Gammerdinger

Among the paintings, photographs, and carvings exhibited in a gallery in Pasco, south-central Washington, are several metal sculptures of branches and leaves, highly detailed in execution, almost fluid in quality. They are the work of the late Walter (Buzz) Culbert, an industrial welder who was employed by the Hanford Reservation, a center for nuclear research and production. Culbert learned to weld in the Seattle shipyards during the 1930s, and at home after work he began "fooling around," making small figures with a welding torch. His sculptures were usually modeled on things that were important to him, such as a baby shoe like his infant son's, or on regional images: a miniature covered wagon, local flowers, mushrooms, fallen logs. The items themselves were aesthetically pleasing, and the challenge of producing them tested his skill with a welding torch.

During World War II, Culbert taught welding in the Seattle shipyards. After the war he moved to Pasco to help build the power plants and experimental facilities that make up the Hanford Reservation. He became an expert in sophisticated welding techniques, and his expertise was often sought by people experimenting with new types of welds or welding difficult metals. During those years of professional growth, Culbert refined his artistry. In the 1970s he made larger welded models, usually of flowers, branches, and leaves, striving for detail and realism, experimenting with colors and textures. His art sparked the interest of other workers at Hanford, and he began teaching his craft to colleagues such as Jacob Stappler, who now enjoys recognition as an artist-welder in the Tri-Cities.

Jacob Stappler of Pasco learned artistic welding from his neighbor and fellow Hanford worker Walter (Buzz) Culbert. Stappler's work is better known in the Tri-Cities area because he has taken the time to market his sculptures and give them public exposure.

Artistic welders belong to a special group of folk artists in Washington: people who use the skills and tools of their trade to create art that reflects their work, and sometimes their personal interests or regional identity as well. Many of them make models of equipment used in their work. For example, Andrew Evich, a fisherman from Bellingham, makes models of fishing boats. He says that he builds each model "just like a real boat, from the keel up," and strives for authenticity, replicating ribs, planking, ballast, interior furnishings, and deck equipment. He has even raided his wife's jewelry box and his daughter's doll house for items of the right size, such as small chains and tiny toilets. Evich enjoys the challenge of creating realistic models, and when building them he confronts some of the problems of building and outfitting a real fishing boat. For example, when Evich modeled a miniature purse seiner after his own boat, he modified the design, making it shorter and wider to afford more work and storage space.

Farmers and ranchers also build models of their work tools, particularly nostalgic recreations of horse-drawn agricultural equipment. Their models are often displayed at county fairs and Grange shows. Carl Guhlke of Lincoln County, a retired farmer, builds models of the horse-drawn plows

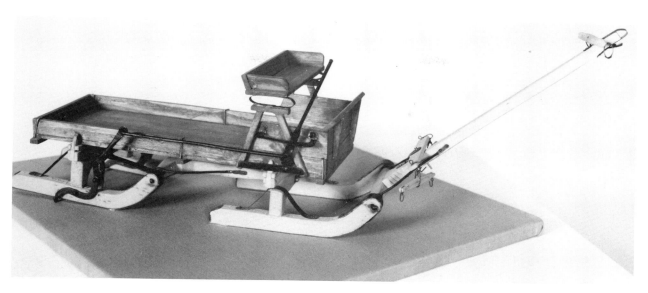

Retired wheat rancher Carl Guhlke of Davenport worked during the era when agriculture made the transition from horsepower to steam to diesel. He had to be a good implement mechanic during these transitions, and he was always interested in the history of agricultural machinery. After his retirement, he put his knowledge to use by documenting the history of farming and transportation and making historically and technically accurate models, which he displays at fairs and Grange shows. Their aesthetic acceptance by his peers is reflected in the many ribbons and certificates he has won for his displays.

he remembers from his father's wheat farm. His most sophisticated piece is a model of a three-blade plow drawn by a twelve-horse team, an exact replica of the plow he and his father used years ago. Guhlke's model not only preserves the design of the equipment, but also commemorates earlier wheat farming in Central and Eastern Washington. The community's appreciation of the model is demonstrated by the numerous ribbons it has won in local fairs and Grange shows.

The late Richard Carl Peterson, like Guhlke, built models with Western

Among the most remarkable woodcarvers in the State of Washington was the late Richard Carl Peterson of Ephrata. Peterson specialized in carving narrative tableaux of frontier and Western scenes, many of them based on true incidents that he heard about or experienced himself. A representation of a Native American killing a grizzly with only a knife (above) was based on an experience of a Blackfoot friend. Peterson was the recipient of a 1988 Governor's Award of Commendation. Scores of his carvings are on display at the Grant County Historical Museum in Ephrata, to which he donated them out of a desire to share his stories with the public.

and agricultural themes. He learned to carve as a boy growing up on a farm in Montana. He characterized his childhood work as "not amounting to much," and he had no time to pursue his interest during his working years. But after he retired from farming and moved to Ephrata, he began carving a wide variety of figures and scenes, most of them Western—cowboys roping, wildlife, agricultural implements. Peterson valued authenticity and took pride in the fact that each of his carvings was "absolutely true," which meant that each depicted a specific event. For example, Peterson knew a Native American in Montana who killed a grizzly bear with a knife. He made several carvings representing this incident, featuring the figure of the wounded grizzly on its hind legs, facing a man with a knife. Peterson regarded the historical verisimilitude of his work as its most important quality.

Peterson made hundreds of carvings after he retired; some of them he displayed in his home, others he gave to family members. About sixty are on exhibit at the Grant County Historical Society in Ephrata: grizzly bears, eagles, hay derricks, and calf ropings. His carvings capture the images that residents feel characterize Central and Eastern Washington. Peterson's contribution to folk art and local heritage was honored when he received the Governor's Award of Commendation in 1988.

Younger folk artists Rod and Jeff Melcher are self-taught cabinetmakers. They are renowned for their elaborate one-twelfth-scale models of wheat ranching machinery—combines, seeders, tractors, and harrows, for example—which they sell all over the Northwest. Their endeavors are financially and artistically successful because they are appreciated by the larger occupational community of Inland Empire wheat ranchers.

Some folk artists honor their professions by creating representations of workers plying their trade, such as the figures of loggers carved by Don Bray. In Washington, logging is one of the most popular subjects of occupational folk art, because of its importance to the state's economy and its long, romantic history. Bray was raised west of Longview, and after working as a pilot and in a pulp mill, he retired to Castle Rock. Bray had always liked to doodle humorous figures, but did not take up woodcarving until he retired and had more spare time. Bray started carving figures he saw in magazines, such as birds and wooden chains. After becoming familiar with woodcarving techniques, he began to draw upon his own experience for subject matter. For his fifty-fifth class reunion, he carved four one-third-scale figures of loggers. In order to get blocks large enough for these figures, which were five feet tall, Bray glued several planks together and then used a chainsaw, a rotary carving tool, knives, and chisels to create the figures. The figures represented the classic specialists of logging as it was done when Bray was young: a faller, a bucker, a high-climber, and a choker-setter. Bray drew upon his own knowledge and the memories of local loggers to make the clothing and equipment historically accurate.

Rod and Jeff Melcher grew up on a wheat ranch in Adams County, between Ritzville and Moses Lake. Both young men are highly skilled cabinetmakers. Their elaborate scale models of modern agricultural equipment have earned them prizes at nearby fairs. Their reputation has spread throughout the Northwest and they are now called upon by wheat ranchers to make models of newly purchased farm machinery. What started as a hobby is now legitimized by public acceptance and by the growing market for the Melcher brothers' work.

Don Olson of Tacoma is a retired logger and civil engineer. After his wife signed him up for an evening-school painting course, he began painting logging scenes. In his early years of working in the woods, loggers still used hand tools to cut timber and steam-powered yarding equipment. Olson's paintings often contrast the technology of logging then and now. His "ghost paintings" illustrate the present-day logger in the foreground, juxtaposed with spectral figures in the same painting, who are using the double-bit axe and the "misery-whip" handsaw of the past.

Logging is also the subject of the art of Don Olson, who worked as a logger until an accident in 1953. He moved to Tacoma, studied drafting, and became a civil engineer for the city. He had always been interested in sketching, so in 1973 his wife gave him painting lessons for Christmas. Olson became an avid painter, focusing on modern logging scenes with their chainsaws and large Caterpillar tractors, and historical scenes featuring hand-buckers and fallers on springboards.

Olson's most distinctive works are his "ghost" paintings, which depict scenes of contemporary loggers at work with ghostly images of earlier loggers in the background performing similar work with hand equipment. With these paintings, Olson commemorates loggers from earlier times, such as his father and grandfather, and recalls the long tradition of logging in the region. Olson's paintings hang in logging supply stores, logging company offices, and in booths at logging shows. His own experience with steam-logging ensures the accuracy of his paintings, and he is critical of painters who may be artistically competent, but put a shackle or guy-wire on the wrong side of a spar tree.

Logging has also inspired the art of chainsaw carving, which grew out of the casual pastime of loggers in the woods who cut figures out of stumps or logs. One of the most accomplished chainsaw carvers in Washington is Otto Oja, a retired bucker and faller living in Cathlamet on the Lower Columbia River. As a youngster, his greatest hero was the logger, and he devotes his talent with wood, music, and drawing to celebrating the logging culture. He writes poetry and songs about logging, is a columnist for

Although Don Bray of Castle Rock was never a logger himself, he grew up around loggers in a timber community and worked for years in a pulp mill. After taking up carving, he was inspired by his logger friends and neighbors to specialize in figures of loggers at work. Most of his figures are about one-third natural size and represent the work of loggers in the days of hand tools and steam yarders. Thus, Bray's work reflects the timber industry's own romanticization of the years before the chainsaw and diesel engine.

Loggers World, plays the harmonica, and draws cartoons about logging. But Oja's greatest interest is in chainsaw carving, which he was inspired to take up after seeing a chainsaw-carved bust of President Kennedy. Since the 1960s, he has taught himself the techniques of carving and has studied anatomy books. Many of his carvings are of loggers working in the woods, holding choker chains and performing other traditional tasks. These realistic and expressive figures are about four feet tall, roughed out with the chainsaw and finished with hand chisels. Oja sells much of his work, mostly in the southwestern part of the state, and sometimes his figures are used as mannequins in logging supply stores. He also enjoys demonstrating chainsaw carving at the logging shows he frequently attends.

Otto Oja of Cathlamet carved this choker-setter. Logger chainsaw artists often depict scenes from work in the woods. Many of Oja's carvings are displayed or even used as mannequins at logging supply stores.

George Flett of Wellpinit is a member of the Spokan Tribe. He is a painter, silversmith, designer, and former museum curator. Flett's reputation as an artist is based in part on his work in sterling silver. He has specialized in making belt buckles and other presentation silver for rodeo awards. "Rodeo silver," as this kind of work is often called, is an important tradition throughout those areas in the American West where rodeo flourishes. Flett's work is unique in the way that it weds an occupational artistic tradition with inspiration from his Native American background. His work is particularly suitable for awards at Indian rodeos.

Wherever cattle are herded from horseback, there is a demand for working saddles and other leather horse gear. One of the leading leatherworkers on Washington's Columbia Plateau is Bob Taylor of Othello. Unlike the saddles made for rodeo and riding competitions, Taylor's work is relatively unembellished. Instead, he emphasizes the craftsmanship of a saddle that will last for years for a working cowboy. But Taylor's saddles (above and at right) are attractive as well as functional, and they must meet both the aesthetic and practical standards of his customers.

Growing up on a cattle ranch near Tucson, Arizona, Alfredo Campos learned to braid rawhide from local cowboys. After moving to Washington (he now lives in Federal Way), he taught himself the Western art of horsehair hitching. He is now an acknowledged master in this field, and has been featured in several national publications. Campos works as a foreman in a Boeing sheet-metal shop.

Ranching, like fishing and logging, has been central to the economy of the state; it has a long, romanticized history, and has inspired many artists who bring to their art the skills they learned on ranches. Saddlemakers, for example, produce saddles for working cowboys and riding enthusiasts. These saddles must be durable and comfortable for both horse and rider, and some saddlers decorate the saddle with leather tooling and silver work.

Ranch life has also inspired the art of horsehair hitching. Alfredo Campos, who now works for Boeing Aircraft as a brake-operator foreman in a sheet-metal shop, grew up on a ranch outside Tucson, Arizona, where he learned how to braid rawhide from family members and working cowboys. After moving to Washington, he learned horsehair hitching, transferring to this new craft the techniques he had used for rawhide braiding, and acquiring new techniques by corresponding with other horsehair braiders.

Campos buys his horsehair from a rendering plant in Stanwood, and dyes it green, red, blue, yellow, and white. He braids the strands together into belts, bridles, quirts, and other riding gear, creating elaborate patterns with the various colors. Campos has built a portable workbench for his hitching, made up of a seat, a light, and a stand that holds the horsehair while he pulls the pieces. Although his work is respected among enthusiasts, he considers himself to be still learning the craft.

This representation of a bass was formerly a catalytic converter on an imported car. It was made by R. J. Burrows at Dean's Muffler and Brake Shop in Ellensburg. Shop owner Dean Curtis began making such pieces in 1980, after seeing them at other shops. When Burrows started working for Curtis in 1984, he too became involved. This kind of work is another example of how occupational skills, in this case welding and cutting, can be adapted to artistic expression. The aesthetics of "muffler art" seem to be shared within the occupational community of automotive repair people; such pieces are often seen in front of shops in many places in the United States.

New art forms have grown out of industrial occupations. In Ellensburg, Dean's Muffler and Brake Shop's front lot is filled with fanciful sculptures made from mufflers, exhaust pipes, used car parts, and other scrap metal. The shop's owner, Dean Curtis, began making these sculptures in 1980. He had seen figures fabricated from exhaust-system parts and decided to give it a try. Using cutting and welding torches, he shapes the scraps into caricatured human and animal figures, and paints them to accentuate the effect. Curtis figures he has made about twenty-five sculptures since he started, working on them mostly in the winter when work in the shop is slow. He gets ideas for the figures by looking at scrap pieces lying around the shop and imagining what they could be made to resemble. Four years ago, R.J. Burrows began working in the shop and he, too, has taken up the art.

Scrap-metal sculpture may seem different from the art inspired by more traditional occupations, but it actually shares the same features: the technical skills, the tools, and the materials typical of the occupation are used to create artifacts, many of which represent the occupation. The resulting art is often admired by members of the community, but may not be recognized as "real art" by outsiders. The artisans are self-taught, or learn techniques by imitation, informal instruction, and practice. The common bond among occupational folk artists is the emotional core of their work, which celebrates their occupation by demonstrating mastery of their tools and skills, and by commemorating the history and traditions of their trade. ❖

BIBLIOGRAPHY

Folk Culture or Folklife, General

Bartis, Peter, ed. *Folklife & Fieldwork: A Layman's Introduction to Field Techniques*. Publications of the American Folklife Center No. 3. Washington, D.C.: Library of Congress, American Folklife Center, 1979.

Bronner, Simon J., ed. *American Material Culture and Folklife*. Ann Arbor, MI: UMI Research Press, 1985.

Brunvand, Jan Harold. *The Study of American Folklore: An Introduction*. Third Edition. New York: W.W. Norton, 1986.

Dorson, Richard M., ed. *Folklore and Folklife: An Introduction*. Chicago: University of Chicago Press, 1972.

_____, and Inta Gale Carpenter, ed. *Handbook of American Folklore*. Bloomington, IN: Indiana University Press, 1983.

Hall, Patricia, and Charlie Seemann. *Folklife and Museums: Selected Readings*. Nashville, TN: American Association for State and Local History, 1987.

Jackson, Bruce, Judith McCulloh, and Marta Weigle. *Folklore/Folklife*. Washington, D.C.: The American Folklore Society, 1984.

Jones, Michael Owen. *The Hand Made Object and Its Maker*. Berkeley: University of California Press, 1975.

Journal of American Folklore (Washington, D.C.). 1888-present.

Journal of Folklore Research, formerly *Journal of the Folklore Institute* (Bloomington, IN). 1963-present.

Western Folklore, formerly *California Folklore Quarterly* (Berkeley, CA). 1941-present.

Folk Culture or Folklife, Northwest

Attebery, Louie, ed. *Idaho Folklife: Homesteads to Headstones*. Salt Lake City: University of Utah Press, 1985.

Jones, Suzi. *Oregon Folklore*. Eugene, OR: University of Oregon, Randall V. Mills Archives of Northwest Folklore, 1977.

_____. "Regionalization: A Rhetorical Strategy." *Journal of the Folklore Institute* 13:1 (1976): 105-20.

Northwest Folklore (Caldwell, ID). 1965-68, 1984-present.

Toelken, Barre. *The Dynamics of Folklore*. Boston: Houghton-Mifflin Co., 1979.

Walls, Robert E., compiler and ed. *Bibliography of Washington State Folklore and Folklife: Selected and Partially Annotated*. Seattle: University of Washington Press for the Washington State Folklife Council, 1987.

White, Sid, and Sam Solberg, ed. *Peoples of Washington*. Pullman: Washington State University Press, 1989.

Folk Art and Craft, General

Ames, Kenneth L. *Beyond Necessity: Art in the Folk Tradition.* New York: W.W. Norton for the Henry Francis du Pont Winterthur Museum, 1977.

Anon. "Folk Art Meeting: Calm and Placid on the Surface . . ." [Library of Congress] *Folklife Center News* 7:1 (January-March 1984): 4-5, 13.

Antiques, The Editors of *The Magazine*, ed. "What Is Folk Art?: A Symposium." *The Magazine Antiques* 57 (1950): 355-62.

Bronner, Simon J. *American Folk Art: A Guide to Sources.* New York: Garland Publishing, 1984.

_____. *Chain Carvers: Old Men Crafting Meaning.* Lexington, KY: The University Press of Kentucky, 1985.

_____. *A Critical Bibliography of American Folk Art.* Bloomington, IN: Folklore Publications Group, 1978.

_____. *Grasping Things: Folk Material Culture and Mass Society in America.* Lexington, KY: The University Press of Kentucky, 1986.

Camp, Charles, ed. *Traditional Craftsmanship in America.* Washington, D.C.: National Council for the Traditional Arts, 1983.

Glassie, Henry. "Folk Art." In *Folklore and Folklife: An Introduction.* ed. Richard M. Dorson, 253-80. Chicago: University of Chicago Press, 1972.

_____. *Pattern in the Material Folk Culture of the Eastern United States.* Philadelphia: University of Pennsylvania Press, 1968.

Loomis, Ormond. *Cultural Conservation: The Protection of Cultural Heritage in the United States.* Washington, D.C.: Library of Congress, American Folklife Center, 1983.

Quimby, Ian M.G., and Scott Schwank, ed. *Perspectives on American Folk Art.* New York: W.W. Norton, 1980.

Sink, Susan. *Traditional Crafts and Craftsmanship in America: A Selected Bibliography.* Washington, D.C.: Library of Congress, American Folklife Center, 1983.

Teske, Robert T. "What is Folk Art? An Opinion on the Controversy." *El Palacio: The Magazine of the Museum of New Mexico* 88 (Winter 1983): 34-38.

Vlach, John Michael. "American Folk Art: Questions and Quandaries." *Winterthur Portfolio* 15 (1980): 245-55.

_____, and Simon J. Bronner. *Folk Art and Art Worlds.* Ann Arbor, MI: UMI Research Press, 1986.

Northwestern Folk Art

Jones, Suzi, ed. *Webfoots and Bunchgrassers: Folk Art of the Oregon Country.* Salem, OR: Oregon Arts Commission and the University of Oregon Museum of Art, 1980.

Martin, Irene, and Janice Queener-Shaw. "Heritage in Wood: Furniture Made by Hand in Western Washington, 1830-1930." [Seattle] *Portage* 7 (1-2): 4-13.

McLachlan, Diana. *A Common Thread . . . Quilts in the Yakima Valley.* Yakima, WA: Yakima Valley Museum and Historical Association, 1985.

Siporin, Steve, ed. *Cityfolk.* Portland: Oregon Arts Commisssion, 1981.

_____, ed. *Folk Art of Idaho: "We Came to Where We Were Supposed to Be."* Boise, ID: Idaho Commission on the Arts, 1984.

Veirs, Kristina, ed. with text by Nancy Hausauer. *Nordic Heritage Northwest.* Seattle: The Writing Works, 1982.

White, Sid. *Chicano and Latino Artists in the Pacific Northwest.* Olympia, WA: The Evergreen State College and Exhibit Touring Services, 1984.

White, Virginia. *Pa Ndau: The Needlework of the Hmong.* Cheney, WA: privately published, 1982.

Williams, Vivian T. "Ag Art: Grange Agricultural Displays." *Seattle Folklore Society Journal* 4:1 (1972): 2-7.

Woolery, Robert L. "The Horsehair Hitching of Alfredo Campos." *Western Horseman*, October 1984: 14-17.

Native American Folk Art, Washington and Northwest

(General)

Baird, Genevieve. *Northwest Indian Basketry.* Tacoma: Washington State American Revolution Bicentennial Commission, 1976.

Jones, Joan M. *The Art and Style of Western Indian Basketry.* Surrey, B.C.: Hancock House, 1982.

(Coastal and Puget Sound)

Ashwell, Greg. *Coast Salish: Their Art, Culture, Legends.* Surrey, B.C.: Hancock House, 1978.

Carlson, Roy L., ed. *Indian Art Traditions of the Northwest Coast.* Burnaby, B.C.: Simon Fraser University Archaeology Press, 1982.

Gunther, Erna. *Art in the Life of the Northwest Coast Indian.* Portland, OR: Portland Art Museum, 1966.

Gustafson, Paula. *Salish Weaving.* Vancouver, B.C.: Douglas and McIntyre, 1980.

Holm, Bill. *Northwest Coast Indian Art: An Analysis of Form.* Seattle: University of Washington Press, 1965.

_____. *Spirit and Ancestor: A Century of Northwest Coast Indian Art at the Burke Museum.* Seattle: University of Washington Press, 1987.

Inverarity, Robert Bruce. *Art of the Northwest Coast Indians.* Berkeley: University of California Press, 1950.

Jones, Joan M. *Northwest Coast Basketry and Culture Change.* Thomas Burke Memorial Washington State Museum, Research Report No. 1. Seattle: University of Washington Press, 1968.

Lobb, Alan. *Indian Baskets of the Northwest Coast.* Portland: Graphic Arts Center Publishing Co., 1978.

Nordquist, D.C., and G.E. Nordquist. *Twana Twined Basketry.* Ramona, CA: Acoma Books, 1983.

Stewart, Hilary. *Cedar: Tree of Life to the Northwest Coast Indians.* Seattle: University of Washington Press, 1984.

Thompson, Nile, and Carolyn Marr. *Crow's Shells: Artistic Basketry of Puget Sound.* Seattle: Dushuyay Publications, 1983.

Whatcom Museum of History and Art, Staff of, ed. *A Report: Master Carvers of the Lummi, and Their Apprentices.* Bellingham, WA: Whatcom Museum of History and Art, 1971.

Wingert, Paul S. *American Indian Sculpture: A Study of the Northwest Coast.* New York: J.J. Augustin Publishers, 1949.

(Plateau)

Gogol, J.M. "Columbia River Indian Basketry." *American Indian Basketry* 1:1 (1979): 4-9.

_____. "Cornhusk Bags and Hats of the Columbia Plateau Indians." *American Indian Basketry* 1:2 (1980): 4-11.

_____. "Elsie Thomas Shows How to Make a Klickitat Indian Basket." *American Indian Basketry* 1:1 (1979): 18-30.

_____. "Rose Frank Shows How to Make a Nez Perce Cornhusk Bag." *American Indian Basketry* 1:2 (1980): 22-31.

Kuneki, Nettie, Elsie Thomas, and Marie Slockish. *The Heritage of Klickitat Basketry: A History and Art Preserved.* Portland: Oregon Historical Society, 1982.

Schlick, Mary. "Art Treasures of the Columbia Plateau." *American Indian Basketry* 1:2 (1980): 12-21.

_____. "Cedar Bark Baskets." *American Indian Basketry* 4:3 (1984): 26-29.

Shackleford, R.S., Mrs. "Legend of the Klickitat Basket." *American Anthropologist* 2:4 (1900): 779-80.

Smith, Marian W. and Harold J. "Basketry Design and the Columbia Valley Art Style." *Southwestern Journal of Anthropology* 8:3 (1952): 336-41.

Wyman, Anne. "Cornhusk Bags of the Nez Perce Indians." *Masterkey* 9:3 (1935): 89-95.

Folk Art, Elsewhere

Cannon, Hal, ed. *Utah Folk Art: A Catalog of Material Culture.* Provo, UT: Brigham Young University Press, 1980.

Dewhurst, C. Kurt, and Marsha MacDowell. *Rainbows in the Sky: The Folk Art of Michigan in the Twentieth Century.* East Lansing: Michigan State University, The Museum, 1988.

_____, Betty MacDowell, and Marsha MacDowell. *Religious Folk Art in America: Reflections of Faith.* New York: E.P. Dutton, 1983.

John Michael Kohler Arts Center, Staff of, ed. *Hmong Art: Tradition and Change.* Sheboygan, WI: John Michael Kohler Arts Center, 1986.

Ohrn, Steven. *Passing Time and Traditions: Contemporary Iowa Folk Artists.* Ames, IA: The Iowa State University Press for the Iowa Arts Council, 1984.

Peterson, Sally. "Translating Experience and the Reading of a Story Cloth." *Journal of American Folklore* 101:399 (January-March 1988): 6-22.

Teske, Robert E., ed. *From Hardanger to Harleys: A Survey of Wisconsin Folk Art.* Sheboygan, WI: John Michael Kohler Arts Center, 1987.

Vlach, John Michael. *The Afro-American Tradition in the Decorative Arts.* Cleveland, OH: Cleveland Museum of Art, 1978. ❖

APPENDIX: ETHNIC RESOURCE GUIDE

By Scott Nagel, Director, Northwest Folklife Festival, Seattle

This selected guide was compiled with assistance from Pat Matheny-White of Exhibit Touring Services. Many of the organizations listed below publish calendars, directories, and catalogs. With a little effort you can find music and dance artists, craftspeople, films, exhibits, lectures, workshops, and other resources for presenting a program or simply becoming better-informed about ethnic Washington.

ORGANIZATIONS

The following organizations have information on a variety of ethnic programs and on hundreds of groups too numerous to list in this guide.

Ethnic Heritage Council of the Pacific
   Northwest
3123 Eastlake E.
Seattle, WA 98102
(206) 726-0055
   Membership includes more than 100 ethnic groups. Publishes a monthly newspaper and annual ethnic heritage directory and offers other programs. Provides referrals and resources for ethnic performers.

Exhibit Touring Services
The Evergreen State College
Olympia, WA 98505
(206) 866-6000 ext. 6075
   A consortium of public and nonprofit exhibiting organizations that provides touring exhibits, including ethnic programs.

Northwest Folkdancer
c/o Linda Caspermeyer
1023 N.E. 61st
Seattle, WA 98115
(206) 525-6143
   Publishes a monthly calendar of folkdance activities.

Northwest Folklife Festival
305 Harrison St.
Seattle, WA 98109
(206) 684-7300
   The Northwest's largest multi-ethnic festival is held in Seattle on Memorial Day weekend and features more than 300 ethnic performing groups. Festival organizers also provide a variety of ethnic and school programs throughout the year, and provide referrals for ethnic performing artists.

Seattle Folklore Society
6556 Palatine Ave. N.
Seattle, WA 98103
(206) 782-0505
   Publishes a monthly newsletter that lists ethnic and folk concerts and dances.

Seattle's Sister Cities
Office of International Affairs
City of Seattle
700 Third Ave., Suite 440
Seattle, WA 98104
(206) 386-1511
   Information on Seattle's thirteen Sister Cities.

The Inquiring Mind: A Forum for the
   Humanities
Washington Commission for the
   Humanities
Lowman Building #312
107 Cherry St.
Seattle, WA 98104
(206) 682-1770
   Offers a variety of programs to community organizations; many of the topics relate to the cultural, social, and economic concerns of ethnic groups.

Victory Music
P.O. Box 7515
Bonney Lake, WA 98390
(206) 863-6617

Publishes a monthly newsletter with listings of ethnic and folk concerts and dances. Offers referral service primarily for folk music and children's programs.

Washington State Folklife Council
7510 Armstrong St. S.W.
Tumwater, WA 98501
(206) 586-8252

The State Folklorist provides a variety of services: primary research on Washington traditions, quarterly newsletter, publications and recordings, referrals to ethnic and traditional artists, and folk art exhibits.

World Affairs Council
Stouffer Madison Hotel, Suite 501
515 Madison St.
Seattle, WA 98104
(206) 682-6986

Offers a variety of programs and resources, including an excellent directory of Asian Pacific Resources.

FILM AND VIDEO

Many excellent films, videotapes, and slide tape programs produced in Washington are widely distributed. Check with your local library and university media center. The following is a selected list of libraries and independent film distributors with extensive holdings.

■ Libraries

Evergreen State College Film Library
Olympia, WA 98505
(206) 866-6000

King County Library Media Center
300 Eighth Ave. N.
Seattle, WA 98109
(206) 684-9000

Seattle Public Library Media Center
1000 Fourth Ave.
Seattle, WA 98104
(206) 386-4662

University of Washington
Instructional Media Services
Kane Hall DG-10
Seattle, WA 98195
(206) 543-9900

Washington State Library
Audio Visual Services
Capitol Campus, AJ-100
Olympia, WA 98504-0111
(206) 753-5590

Washington State University Media Center
Pullman, WA 99164-5610
(509) 335-4557

■ Film Distributors-Northwest

Film Distribution Center
13500 N.E. 124th St.
Kirkland, WA 98034
(206) 820-2592

University of Oregon
Folklore and Ethnic Programs
Eugene, OR 97403
(503) 686-3911
(*Northwest/International*)

Northwest Film and Video Center
1219 S.W. Park Ave.
Portland, OR 97205
(503) 221-1156
(*International*)

Oregon Historical Society
1230 S.W. Park Ave.
Portland, OR 97205
(503) 222-1741
(*Primarily Northwest*)

■ Film Distributors-National

Appalshop Films
P.O. Box 743
306 Madison St.
Whitesburg, KY 41858
(800) 545-7467
(*Appalachian*)

Bayou Films
Route 3 Box 614
Cut Off, LA 70345
(504) 632-4100
(*Louisiana/Southern*)

Flower Films
10341 San Pablo Ave.
El Cerrito, CA 94530
(415) 525-0942
(*Films of Les Blank and Others;
     Ethnic and Eclectic*)

One West
535 Cordova Road, Suite 410
Santa Fe, NM 87501
(505) 983-8685
(*The American West*)

Public Media, Inc.
535 Cordova Road, Suite 200
Santa Fe, NM 87501
(505) 982-4757
(*Primarily Southwest*)

Rhapsody Films
P.O. Box 179
New York, NY 10014
(212) 243-0152
(*Primarily Jazz and Blues*)

MUSEUMS AND HISTORICAL SOCIETIES

There are more than 400 museums and historical societies throughout the state. The Washington Museum Association (P.O. Box 6549, Bellevue, WA 98008, (206) 333-4575) publishes a complete directory. Contact your local Chamber of Commerce or library for the organization nearest to you.

■ **State Historical Societies**

Eastern Washington State Historical
   Society
2316 First Ave.
Spokane, WA 99204
(509) 456-3931

Washington State Capital Museum
211 W. 21st Ave., KM-11
Olympia, WA 98504
(206) 753-2580

Washington State Historical Society
Hewitt Library
315 N. Stadium Way
Tacoma, WA 98403
(206) 593-2830

■ **Selected List of Ethnic Museums**

Black Diamond Historical Museum
32627 Baker, P.O. Box 232
Black Diamond, WA 98010
(206) 886-1168

Colville Cultural Center
P.O. Box 150
Nespelem, WA 99155
(509) 634-4711

Colville Tribes Museum
P.O. Box 233
Coulee Dam, WA 99116
(509) 633-0751

Daybreak Star Indian Cultural Center
Discovery Park, P.O. Box C99305
Seattle, WA 98199
(206) 285-4425

Fort Spokane Museum
National Park Service
P.O. Box 37
Coulee Dam, WA 99116
(509) 633-0881

Fort Walla Walla Museum
Myra Road, P.O. Box 1616
Walla Walla, WA 99362
(509) 525-7703

Historisches Museum
Fourth and Elm Streets, P.O. Box 536
Odessa, WA 99159
(509) 982-2539

Makah Cultural and Research Center
East Front St., P.O. Box 95
Neah Bay, WA 98357
(206) 645-2711

Museum of Native American Cultures
E. 200 Cataldo
Spokane, WA 99202
(509) 326-4550

Nordic Heritage Museum
3014 N.W. 67th St.
Seattle, WA 98117
(206) 789-5707

Sacajawea Interpretive Center
Sacajawea State Park, RR9 - Box 2503
Pasco, WA 99301
(509) 545-2361

Samish Coastal Cultural Center
Samish Indian Tribe
P.O. Box 217
Anacortes, WA 98221
(206) 293-6404

Snoqualmie Tribal Museum
18525 Novelty Road
Redmond, WA 98052
(206) 885-7464

Steilacoom Tribal Museaum
1515 Lafayette St.
Steilacoom, WA 98388
(206) 584-6308

Suquamish Museum
Sandy Hook Road, P.O. Box 498
Suquamish, WA 98392
(206) 598-3311

Tulalip Tribal Museum
6700 Totem Beach Road
Marysville, WA 98270
(206) 653-4585

Yakima Nation Museum
Hwy. 97, P.O. Box 151
Toppenish, WA 98498
(509) 865-2800

Wing Luke Asian Museum
414 Eighth Ave. S.
Seattle, WA 98104
(206) 623-5124

ETHNIC/FOLK ARTS FESTIVALS

The following is a selected list of ethnic and multi-ethnic festivals sponsored by a variety of ethnic and cultural organizations. The events are arranged in chronological order for 1989. Call or write to confirm details, because dates and other information can change from one year to the next.

January—Seattle
The American Brazilian Society Carnival
TABS
20014 103rd Ct. N.E.
Bothell, WA 98011
(206) 485-3500
Costume contest, traditional food, music and dance.

February—Seattle Center
Sundiata
907 Pine St., Suite 701
Seattle, WA 98101
(206) 467-8656
A celebration of Black culture, art, and history, including music and dance performances, films, and workshops.

March—Seattle Center
Irish Festival
Irish Heritage Club
18317 Evanston Ave. N.
Seattle, WA 98133
(206) 747-9887
Irish singers, dance performances, workshops, and film festival.

April—Seattle Center
Cherry Blossom Japanese Cultural Festival
(206) 684-7200
Demonstrations of martial arts, calligraphy, and Ikebana, along with traditional music, dance, films, and art.

April—Oak Harbor
Holland Happening
P.O. Box 883
Oak Harbor, WA 98277
(206) 675-3535
Traditional music, dance, food, and flower displays.

April—Pacific Lutheran University, Tacoma
Norwegian Heritage Festival
Jim Kittilsby, Office of Development
Pacific Lutheran University
Tacoma, WA 98447
(206) 535-8797
Traditional Norwegian foods, crafts, and demonstrations.

April—Northgate Mall, Seattle
Ethnic Fest
Ethnic Heritage Council
3123 Eastlake E.
Seattle, WA 98102
(206) 726-0055
A variety of ethnic crafts, foods, music, and dance.

May—Lynden
Holland Days Festival
P.O. Box 647
Lynden, WA 98264
(206) 354-5995
   Authenic Klompen dancers, Dutch arts, crafts, and food.

May—Church of the Assumption, Seattle
Greek Village Festival
1804 13th Ave.
Seattle, WA 98102
(206) 485-8943
   Greek food, dancing, church tours, bazaar.

May—Seattle Center
Northwest Folklife Festival
Scott Nagel
305 Harrison St.
Seattle, WA 98109
(206) 684-7300
   The Northwest's largest multi-ethnic festival with nineteen stages and more than 700 performing groups, craftspeople, food, films, and more.

May—Soap Lake
Greek Festival
P.O. Box 433
Soap Lake, WA 98851
(509) 246-0462
   Traditional food, dancing, and music.

June—Toppenish
Treaty Days
Yakima Nation Museum
P.O. Box 151
Toppenish, WA 98498
(509) 865-2800
   Annual celebration with Native American music, dance, storytelling, food, and videos, all at the Cultural Center and Museum.

June—Frank Rabb Park, Poulsbo
Skandia Midsommar Fest
1612 N. 53rd St.
Seattle, WA 98103
(206) 633-4225
   Scandinavian dance, music, food, arts and crafts.

June-July—Bluegrass Park, Darrington
Darrington Bluegrass Festival
Samuel H. Nations
26429 469th Ave. N.E.
Darrington, WA 98241
(206) 436-1077
   A weekend of bluegrass music in Washington's leading "Tarheel" community.

June-July (even-numbered years)—Naselle
Finnish-American Folk Festival
Anna Erlund (206) 484-7759
Susan Pakanen-Holway (206) 484-3848
P.O. Box 146
Naselle, WA 98638
   A celebration of Finnish traditions.

June-August—Spokane
Festival of Four Cultures
311 Riverside Ave.
Spokane, WA 99201
(509) 624-3605
   A summer-long program honoring Asian, European, Old West, and Native American cultures.

July—Seattle Center
1989 Sangerfest
1513 Debrelon Lane
Mukilteo, WA 98275
(206) 347-2769
   Nearly 1,000 male singers participate in this Norwegian songfest.

July—Seattle Center
Naturalization Ceremony
Ethnic Heritage Council of the Pacific
   Northwest
3123 Eastlake E.
Seattle, WA 98102
(206) 726-0055
   Over 500 new American citizens are sworn in during a public, official ceremony sponsored by the Ethnic Heritage Council of the Pacific Northwest.

July—Spokane
Pinesong
Spokane Falls Community College
W3410 Ft. George Wright Dr., MS 3020
Spokane, WA 99204
(509) 459-3800
   A weekend-long folk music festival that often includes storytellers and poets.

July—Nordic Heritage Museum, Seattle
Tivoli
3014 N.W. 67th St.
Seattle, WA 98117
(206) 789-5707
    Nordic crafts, music, and dance.

July—Seattle
Chinatown-International District Summer
    Festival
International District Association
P.O. Box 3152
Seattle, WA 98104
(206) 725-1842
    Music, dance ensembles, and food are
included in this day-long festival celebrating the diversity of the Chinatown-International District.

July—Stevenson
Skamania Bluegrass and Country Music
    Festival
P.O. Box 1037
Stevenson, WA 98648
(509) 427-8911
    Music, food, and dancing; camping on
the grounds with advance registration.

July—Whitman Mission, Walla Walla
Whitman Mission Powwow
Rt 2. Box 247
Walla Walla, WA 99362
(509) 522-6360
    Dancing, drumming, and singing are
featured in this celebration of Native
American culture.

July—Seattle Buddhist Church
Bon Odori
1427 S. Main St.
Seattle, WA 98144
(206) 329-0800
    A Japanese folkdance festival with
traditional arts and food.

July—King County Fairgrounds,
    Enumclaw
Pacific Northwest Scottish Highland
    Games
SSHGA
P.O. Box 246
Enumclaw, WA 98022
(206) 522-2874
    A weekend of traditional Scottish
music, dancing, and athletic competition.

July—Seward Park, Seattle
Hispanic SeaFair Festival
414 Pontius Ave N., Suite C
Seattle, WA 98109
(206) 296-3824
    Latino music and food in celebration
of Latin American culture.

August—Suquamish
Chief Seattle Days
P.O. Box 498
Suquamish, WA 98392
(206) 598-3311
    Traditional arts and crafts, salmon
dinner, dancing, and powwow in
celebration of Chief Seattle.

August—Usk
Native American Cultural Fair
P.O. Box 389
Usk, WA 99180
(509) 445-1147
    Traditional arts, crafts, and food at this
Kalispel/Salish fair.

August—Neah Bay
Makah Days
P.O. Box 507
Neah Bay, WA 98357
(206) 645-2063
    Traditional food, dancing, and canoe
racing at the annual celebration of 1913
flag-raising and 1924 citizenship.

September—Seattle Center
Fiesta Patrias
Concilio for the Spanish Speaking
157 Yesler Way, Suite 209
Seattle, WA 98104
(206) 461-4891
    A celebration of Mexican and Latin
independence with traditional food, music,
and dance.

September—Odessa
Odessa Deutsches Fest
P.O. Box 65
Odessa, WA 99159
(509) 982-0049
    Food, beer, and entertainment in the
German tradition.

September—Kelso
Kelso Highlander Festival
300 Oak St.
Kelso, WA 98626
(206) 636-3300
  Bagpipe bands, Highlander games, and food in the Scottish tradition.

September—Seattle
Chilean Independence Day
Celebrate Central America
P.O. Box 4220
Seattle, WA 98104

September—Ritzville
Mennonite Country Auction
Menno Mennonite Church
Rt. 1 Box 91
Ritzville, WA 99169
(509) 765-8683
  An auction of quilts, German food, demonstrations of skills, and other community activities.

October—St. Demetrios Church, Seattle
St. Demetrios Greek Festival
2100 Boyer Ave. E.
Seattle, WA 98112
(206) 325-4347
  Greek dancing, food (including complete dinners and to-go), music, church tours, crafts, and more.

October—Puyallup
Scandinavian Festival
314 18th St. N.W.
Puyallup, WA 98371
(206) 845-5446
  Twenty-fifth annual event sponsored by Leif Erickson Memorial committee. Celebration of Scandinavian culture including exhibits, music, arts and crafts, food, and folkdancing.

October—Seattle
Festa Italiana
10800 N.E. Eighth St., #1015
Bellevue, WA 98004
(206) 454-6024
  A celebration of Italian heritage, especially food.

October—Walla Walla
Italian Heritage Days
Walla Walla Italian Heritage Society
P.O. Box 752
Walla Walla, WA 99362
(509) 525-1021
  A celebration of food, music, agriculture, and dance in Washington's oldest Italian community.

November—Seattle Center
Hmong New Year
P.O. Box 1622
Seattle, WA 98118
(206) 684-7200
  Traditional New Year celebration.

December—Seattle
Filipino Youth Activities Carnival
FYA Center
810 18th Ave.
Seattle, WA 98122
(206) 323-6545

December—Anacortes
St. Nicholas Croatian Celebration
P.O. Box 6
Anacortes, WA 98221
(206) 293-6211
  The Vela Luka Croatian Dance Ensemble performs and traditional foods are served at this Christmas celebration. Multi-ethnic music, dancing, food, and crafts.

December—Lynden
Dutch Sinterklass Celebration
P.O. Box 647
Lynden, WA 98264
(206) 354-5995
  Traditional Dutch Christmas celebration with Klompen dancing, food, and carols.

December
Seattle—Ano Nuevo Latino Americano
Casa Chile
P.O. Box 4220
Seattle, WA 98104
(206) 363-8242
  New Year's Eve celebration with traditional Latino music, dance, food, and crafts.

INDEX

Numbers in italics refer to photographs

A

Aberdeen, 36, 39, 45
Abrahamson, Cecilia, *47*
Adams County, 30
African-Americans, 4
Agricultural workers, 2, 5, 7
Alaska, 5, 7, 36, 45
Anderson, Al, 64, *64*
Anderson, Nikolas, 64
Anderson, Nora, 64, *64*
Annual Western Art Show and Auction,
    Ellensburg, 32
Appalachians, 2
Arizona, 29, 90
Arlington, 58
Asians, xii, 2, 5

B

Baby-boards, 63
Baloney Joe's, 76
Basketmaking, *12*, 20, *21*, 22, 45-46, *52, 55,*
    57-59, *60*
Battle Ground, 13, 76
Beadwork, *47*, 63
Bedal, Edith, 59, *60*
Bellingham, 70, 72, 76, 80
Benner, Adam, *36*
Bicentennial, U.S., 74
Birdhouses, 38-39
Black, Margie, *57*
Blacks. *See* African-Americans
Blaine, 74
Bland, Lyle, *17*
Bray, Don, 83, *86*
Bremerton, 1, 58, 80
Bremner, Marie Bakke, *9*, 29, *30*

Bridgeport, 11
British, 2
British Columbia, 5, 36
Broadbent, Floyd, *vi*, 45
Burrows, R.J., 91

C

Cabinetmaking, 38, 83
California, 7
Cambodian Buddhist Temple of Tacoma,
    58, *59*
Cambodians, 5, 58
Campbell, Chuck, 61-62
Campos, Alfredo, *26*, 29, 90, *90*
Canada, 5, 7, 10, 45
Canning, *10*, 13, 72
Canoes, *34*
Carving, *vi, x, xx, 3, 15-17,* 20, 22, *22, 25,*
    28, 33, *33-35,* 35-37, 39, 45-46, *56,* 58,
    61-62, *82,* 83, *86,* 87; chainsaw, *ii, 24,*
    30, 35-36, 49, 61-62, 83, 86-87, *87*
Cascade Range, 4, 7
Castle Rock, 83
Cathlamet, 86
Central America, xiii, 7
Central Park, Washington, 39
Ceramics, 20
Chamberlain, Robert, 33
Chicanos, 2. *See also* Hispanics
Chinese, 2, 22, 27
Clockmaking, *56*
Colfax, Greg, *35*
Columbia River, 45, 86
Colvin, Vada, *7*
Cowboys. *See* Ranching
Cowlitz County, 2
Croatians, 2, 72

Crocheting, 13, 58, 63, 72, *75*
Cromwell, 65
Culbert, Walter (Buzz), 10, *78*, 79
Curtis, Dean, *xii*, 91, *91*

D

Dalmatians. *See* Croatians
Dance. *See* Folkdancing
Darrington, 58-59
Daughters of Norway, 63, 65
Dean's Muffler and Brake Shop,
    Ellensburg, 91
Decoys, *16*, 20
Demus, Lida, *9*
DeWitt, Clarence, 13, *14*
Dollmaking, apple-head, *32;*
    cornhusk, 53, *54*
Dressmaking, *8*, 13, 46, 70
Drummaking, 63
Dutch, 2, 72

E

Easter eggs, *15*, 22
Ellensburg, 32, 91
Embroidery, *8-9*, 13, 46, 74
Emerson, Elene, 63, 65
Engfer, John, 45, *52*, 56-57
Environmental folk art. *See* "Yard art"
Ephrata, 83
Evich, Andrew, *71*, 72, 80

F

Farming. *See* Ranching
Federal Way, 29
Fiddle making. *See* Hardanger fiddles
Fiddling, 13
Filipinos, 2, 5, 7
Finnish-American Folk Festival, Naselle,
    76
Finns, 2, 20, 33, 39, 45, 70
Fishing, commercial, xiii, 2, 7, 45-46, 53,
    70, 72, 80, 90; sports, 1, 13, 22, 67
Flett, George, *88*
Flower-drying, 29
Fly-tying, 13, *14, 66*, 67-70
"Folk art environments." *See* "Yard art"
Folk art, definitions of, xiv, 13-30
Folkdancing, xiv, 39, 46
Folk music, xiv, 16-17, 39, 41, 45-46, 51, 86
Folktales. *See* Storytelling

French-Canadians, 2
Fruit box labels, 33, 50-51
Fruit growing, 7, 33, 50
Fryberg, Raymond, Sr., 63
Furniture making, *viii, 36-37*

G

Gehrke, Emil, *41*
German-Russians, 2, 38
Germans, 2, 57, 74
Gibson, Pat I., *16*
Gifford, Woodrow, 42-43
Gillaspie, Enola Paddock, 74
Glad Tidings Assembly of God,
    Darrington, 58
Graffiti, 13
Granges, 20, 29, 54, 80
Grant County Historical Society, 83
Graves, Monad, *8*
Greeks, 2
Gregory, Elvira Williams, *76-77*
Gross, John, *viii*
Grytness, Dawn, 13, *14*, *66*, 67-70
Guhlke, Carl, 80-82, *81*

H

Hageland, Thorleif (Tom), *56*, 58
Hanford, 2, 79
Hardanger fiddles, *26*, *62*, 63
Hardangersøm, 29, *30*, 63
Hardingfele. See Hardanger fiddles
Harrison, Doug, *xx*, 1, 3, 22
Hartbauer, K.E., *24*
Hays, Finley and Jean, 41
"Heavy metal" music, 13
Hempel, Ida Kooy, 72
"High context" communities, 6-7
Hispanics, xiii, 7. *See also* Chicanos,
    Mexicans
Hmong, 5, 28, 46
Holm, Hazel, 58
Horsehair hitching, *26*, 29, 90, *90*
"Hot rodders," 13
Hunting, 1, 20, 22, 33, 53
Hutterites, 5, 38

I

Idaho, 1, 68
Ilwaco, 70
Indians. *See* Native Americans

Indrebo, Emile S., *26*, *62*, 63-65
Indrebo, Solveig, *62*, 63-65
Irish, 4
Italians, 2, 45

J

Japanese, 2, 4, 22, 27
Japanese-Hawaiians, 29
Jews, 2
Jiménez, Petra, *8*, 46
Johnson, Dena Hobbelink Huisman, 72
Johnson, Elsie Koehler, *4*, *28*, 29
Jones, Stan, Sr., 63

K

Kalama River, 68
Kalama, 13
Kauha, *24*
Kelso, 2
King County, 57
Kittitas County, 20
Knifemaking, *24*
Knitting, 63, 72
Knot-tying. *See* Ropework
Koreans, 5
Korge, 64
Kornyk, John, *15*
Kuneki, Nettie, *21*

L

Lacemaking, *7*, 13, 72, *75*
Landscaping, 38-39
Laotians, 5
Laubsägerarbeit. *See* Scroll-sawing
Lewis County, 2, 41
Lincoln County, 80
Loggers World, 41, 87
Logging, xiii, 1-2, 6, 10, 29-30, 37-39, 41,
    49, 51, 59, 63, 68, 83, 86-87, 90
Long Beach Peninsula, 33
Longview, 2, 74, 83
Loupe, 64
Lugnet, Theodore (Tete), *69*, 70
Lynden, 72
Lynden Pioneer Museum, 74

M

Mahaffey Camp Store, Kalama River, 67

Makah Tribe, 36
Manchester, Blanche Anderson, 70-71
Marquand, Fred, *23*, 76-77
Martha Circle, United Congregational
    Church, Naselle, 76
Marys Corner, 41
Marysville, 61
Masks, *34*
McMeekin, John O., *38*, 39
Melcher, Rod and Jeff, 30, 83, *84*
Merrill, Pete, *40*
Metalwork. *See* Welding
Mexicans, 2, 5, 46
Mexico, 7
Mien, 5, 28
Migrant workers. *See* Agricultural
    workers
Mining, 4, 10, 74
Model-building, 20, 29, 37, *71*, 72, *73*, 74,
    80-83, *81*, *84*
"Mole chasers." *See* Windmills, model
Molson, 29
Montague, Hazel Thompson, 70
Montana, 83
Montesano, 63
Morgan, Lucille, *57*
Morris, Faye, *11*
"Muffler art," *xii*, 91, *91*
Music. *See* Folk music

N

Naches, 45
Naselle, 76, 78
Native Americans, xiii-xiv, 2, 5, 15, 20, 22,
    27, 39, 45-49, 58-59, 61-63, 65, 83;
    Coastal and Puget Sound, xiv, 2, 33,
    36; Plateau, 2
Needlework, 5, 22, 27-29, 72, 76
North Carolina, 2
North Central Washington District Fair,
    Waterville, 20
Norwegians, 2, 22, 29, 46-49, 63-65
Nuclear industry, 2, 10, 79

O

Oja, Otto, *ii*, 35, 86-87, *87*
Okanogan, the, 20
Okanogan County, 29
Oklahoma, 2
Olson, Don, 33, *85*, 86
Olympic Range, 7
Oregon, 35, 68

Oroville, 29
Orting, 45-57
Osusky, Karol, *37*
Ota, Kimi, 27, *27*

P

Pa ndau. See *Paj ntaub*
Pablo, Shannon, 63
Painting, 20, 32-33; logger genre, 32-33,
     85, 86
Paj ntaub, 5, 46, *48*, 49
Palouse, the, 32
Pan-Indianism, 39,46
Parquetry, *36*
Pasco, 10, 79
Person, Dorothy Wooldridge, *10*, 13, *74-
     75*, 76-77
Peterson, Kathy, 58
Peterson, Richard Carl, *22*, 82-83, *82*
Pierce County, 2, 57-58, 64
Pike Place Market, Seattle, 46
Poetry, xiv, 41, 51; cowboy, 41, 51; logger,
     41-43, *44*, 51, 86
Portland, Oregon, 76
Posters, 13
Powell, Betsy, 11
Powwows, 39, 45-46, 61, 63
Pritchard, Al, 68
Puget Sound, 39, 45
"Punkers," 13
"Puyallup Fair." *See* Western Washington
     State Fair
Puyallup Tribe, 36, 63
Puyallup Valley, 56-57

Q

Quaempts, Sarah Albert, *21*
Quileute Tribe, 36
Quilting, *9*, 10, *18*, 20, 28-29, *30*, 39, *57*, 58,
     70, 72, 74, *74*, 76-77; *Sashiko*, 27, *27*
Quincy, 11

R

Ranching, 1, 7, 37, 51, 57, 74, 80, 83, 90;
     cattle, 2; wheat, xiii, 30, 32, 53, 82-83
Rawhide braiding, 29, 90
Raymond, 36
Republic, 29
Richland, 13
Roberts, Betty, 29, *31*

Roberts, Lloyd, 29, *31*
"Rodeo silver." *See* Silversmithing
Rodia, Simon, 17
Ropework, *69*, 70
Rosemaling, 49
Rugs, crocheted, 58, 72; woven, *11*, 74, 76
Russell, Betty Robertson, 70, 72, 74

S

Saddlemaking, 20, *88-89*, 90
Salvadorans, 5
Sauk Tribe, 59
Scandinavians, 2, 38, 63, 65
Schole, Don, *24*, 29-30
Scottish, 2
Scrap-metal sculpture. *See* "Muffler art"
Scroll-sawing, *x*
Seattle, 2, 4, 46, 59, 79
Seaview, 42
Seed art, *4*, 20, *28*, 29
Shelton, 33
Shipping, 76-77
Shipyard work, 10, 79
Silversmithing, *88*, 90
Singing. *See* Folk music
Skagit County, 2
Snohomish County, 2
Soap Lake, 53
Sonntag, Christine, *57*
Sons of Norway, 65
Southeast Asians, 4, 28
Spinning, 29, 63
Spinning wheels, 29, *31*
"Spirit flags." See *Tuong proleang*
Spokane, 39, 46
Square dancing, 13
Stanwood, 90
Stappler, Jacob, 10, 79, *80*
Stieber, Otto Franz, *x*, *73*, 74, 76
"Story cloths." See *Paj ntaub*
Storytelling, xiv, 16-17, 39-41
Suquamish Tribe, 36
Swalander, Frank, *55*, 57
Swan, Bill, *33*
Swanaset, George, *34*
Swedes, 2, 70

T

Tacoma, 4, 33, 58, 63-64, 86
"Talking staffs," *34*
"Tarheels." *See* Appalachians
Tatting, *7*, 13, 58

Tattooing, *23, 77*
Taylor, Bob, *88-89*
Texas, 2
Thais, 5
Tidd, "Blackie," 68
Tine, 64, *64*
Toppenish, 46
Totem poles, 36-37, 61-63
Tri-Cities, 4, 79
Tulalip Treaty Festival, 61
Tulalip Tribe, 20, 36, 61-63, 65
Tuong proleang, 19, 58, *59*

U

Ukrainians, 22
Underwood, Hazel, *12*
United Congregational Church, Naselle,
    76

V

Vancouver, Washington, 30
Vietnamese, 5
Volga Germans. *See* German-Russians

W

Walla Walla, 45
Washington Old Time Fiddlers'
    Association, 13
Waterville, 20
Wauna, 64

Wayside crosses, *37*
Weaving, *6,* 29; cornhusk, *21*
Welding, 10, *78,* 79, *80,* 91
West-to-East Covered Wagon Train, 74
Western Washington State Fair, Puyallup,
    57
Whatcom County, 74-76
"Whirligigs." *See* Windmills, model
Whitmore, Ada, 53, *54*
Whittling. *See* Carving
Willamette Valley, 2
Willapa Hills, 7
Williams, Clyde, Sr., 61
Williams, Cy, 61-62, *61*
Windmills, model, 29, 39, *40-41*
Wirkkala, Ikey, *44*
Wirkkala, Maria, *6*
Wirkkala, Oiva, *25,* 39
Wuorinen, Laura, *32*

X

Xiong, See, *48*
Xiong, Yang Mee, *5, 48*

Y

Yakima, 1
Yakima Regional Woodcarvers
    Association,1
Yakima Valley, 2, 46
Yamamoto, Bette, *18*
"Yard art," 29, 38, *38*
Yugoslavians. *See* Croatians

PHOTO CREDITS